Master the art of colour

Practical Advice from the Room Renovations Expert

Tash Bradley of Lick

Quadrille

Introduction

This book isn't just for the decorating community, it's by the decorating community.

Because everything I've learned about colour and design has been shaped by the conversations I've had with so many of you – whether that's face to face on one of the 5,000 colour consultations I've worked on to date, or via DMs on Lick's social media channels.

It's the shoppers I've spoken to at our London showroom (aka my happy place), and at our concessions in the British DIY store B&Q, who have shared their decorating dilemmas with me and left feeling empowered over which colours to choose in their scheme.

It's the experts I've collaborated with on special ranges, pushing me to create new colours and palettes to evoke a specific mood that represents their campaign, which I might not have come to otherwise.

I love what I do because yes, I love colour and design - but I LOVE helping people, and this is the way I can do that most effectively. I'm always quick to point out that I'm not here to tell anybody what to do, or lead with a particular aesthetic – for me working with clients is very much a collaboration. I always learn something new from every interaction I have with a client, and getting to understand people's common dilemmas is incredibly important in informing my practice.

And it was talking to so many of you that fuelled my desire to distil these learnings into one easily accessible place: the book you're now reading. I wanted to offer the whole story from start to finish, so you can effectively become your own colour consultant and learn how to assess and choose colour with confidence (whatever those colours may be). Through this book I've created a clear, digestible framework for you to follow, which will help you understand what your colour personality is, which colour schemes might suit you best, and how to adapt this to work in the different rooms in your home, before we finally pull everything together to create specific room schemes.

You can almost jump in and out of this book as you like and it'll still make sense: the first two chapters go into detail about colour psychology and how it works, while later on we'll have more of a play with combining colours before we move onto moodboard creation and DIY techniques – so if you're in a rush to get some practical advice, skip to chapter six (but please do come back to read the earlier chapters – I promise you, it's absolutely fascinating).

Let's dive in!

About me

I grew up immersed in the interiors world thanks to my mother, who was (and still is) a brilliant interior designer. We moved house regularly as she renovated then sold a number of our family homes, which for young-me was all one big design adventure. My sisters and I were all allowed to choose our own decor for our bedrooms – and as we moved so often, I was already a bit of a bedroom-decorating pro by the time I left home.

I still have fond memories of her taking me to London's Design Centre, Chelsea Harbour (a go-to destination for many interior designers and architects). I loved flipping through all the sample books of beautiful wallpapers and stunning fabrics, igniting my imagination.

Whilst I've always been passionate about design, I initially pursued a career as a fine artist before moving into brand marketing and events. There, I began to appreciate the power of colour and design in influencing our thoughts and moods (which is a crucial aspect of how brands use their design to entice their customers).

I thrived working in such a social, fast-paced environment, and collaborating with my clients on projects they loved, which got me thinking about how I could find a similar dynamic within the home design sector.

So in my late twenties I headed back to university to study interior design. I loved immersing myself into this world, but it wasn't until we got to a module about colour that I had my lightbulb moment. It fascinated me, and opened my mind to all the amazing and unexpected ways colour influences us, from our food and clothing choices to the colours we paint on our walls. I became totally obsessed with colour, and I knew immediately that this was where I wanted to focus my career.

This all coincided serendipitously with the launch of Lick, so I ended up in the very fortunate position of getting to shape my dream job. And as the business got up and running, I began working on my first Lick client colour consultations. If I'm honest, I felt like a total imposter at the start, and I often referred back to design books and course notes to help me figure

out how I could give the best advice. But this head-first approach really paid off, and I quickly reached a point where I could look at any room and fairly easily figure out how I could help my client achieve the look and feel they wanted. This also helped me refine my process and start to develop a framework for these methods, which has ultimately become this book.

I still can't believe I get paid to spend my days chatting to people about colour – it's safe to say I've found my vocation!

My personal style

If someone met me and then visited my home, I'm pretty sure they'd know instantly it was mine. And for me that's so important, as I really believe our homes should reflect our personalities. My style is colourful (of course!) but cohesive: I like colours and palettes that sit quite tonally together, rather than clashes. I love decorating with pieces that tell a story and over the years I've amassed an eclectic mix of ornaments and artwork filled with memories that make me and my husband happy.

Photo: @emmalewisphotographer

About Lick

Colour can bring us so much joy, but shopping for paint can easily tip into an anxiety-inducing ordeal when faced with a sea of 300 near-identical beiges. The process can also feel quite disjointed: how are you meant to KNOW which of those 300 beiges is right for you – and what you should pair it with – especially when there's nothing or no one really to give you a steer?

This inspired the launch of Lick in 2020, co-founded by Lucas London and my husband Sam, with the aim of better serving today's modern consumer. To simplify the process we launched with a carefully-curated colour palette, which we keep at around 100 colours, and straightforward naming conventions to reduce confusion. So if you're looking for blue, you just need to look for the colours called (yep, you guessed it) blue! (Plus corresponding numbers at the end.)

And we've made sure it's really clear what the tone, character and mood of each colour is on our website (lick.com) – so if you're looking for a blue that feels light and fresh, you can quickly whittle it down to a few key choices.

We've tried to make sample testing as simple as possible, too: we were one of the first brands to develop peel and stick colour samples, saving time and offering a more environmentally friendly (and less messy) alternative to tester pots.

As Director of Interiors at Lick, I curate our colour palettes, which blends my art background and insights from chats I've had with top interior designers and magazine editors, so I really understand what people are looking for. And as a result of all the client colour consultations I've had, I feel in tune with what my customers want in their homes. This, in turn, informs any new colours we create, which is such a lovely circular relationship.

I LOVE to chat about all things colour, and helping people find their perfect palette is such a passion of mine, so if after this book you're still feeling stuck, remember there's plenty more advice on our website and social channels, and my DMs are always open.

Context

When we launched Lick in Spring 2020 as a small (but mighty) team, our focus from day one was to create a community of colour lovers (like us!) and build the business around these relationships, keeping this community element at its core. We could see from the start there was a unique opportunity to directly support and inspire our customers in ways our competitors weren't really able to, which felt really exciting.

And we certainly set off with a bang: our first day of trading actually coincided with the start of the UK's first pandemic-induced lockdown (when most DIY stores – among many other retailers – were forced to close). But as Lick was conceived as online-only to start with, we were able to launch more or less as planned (in fact, as the only direct-to-consumer paint brand in the UK at that time, for our first few weeks of trading we were literally the only place to buy paint – right when many of us found ourselves spending far more time at home, and looking for things to do).

This period drastically changed how we shop for paint, and today the option of buying your preferred paint either online or in-person is pretty standard, which also makes it far more accessible for those who can't easily visit big DIY stores. It was fascinating to be part of the industry during this pivotal shift, and we continue to be extremely grateful to everyone who has supported Lick from both the start and as we've grown – from the team of incredibly hard-working people who helped make it all happen to our amazing Lick community, both globally and locally.

Our signature colours

I know how overwhelming choosing colours can be, so I've worked really hard to ensure every Lick colour works brilliantly on its own, as well as pairing beautifully with each other. This collection below represents what's consistently popular with the Lick community, and what my clients gravitate towards in their homes:

RED 03

A soft versatile red (thanks to its dusky pink undertones), the Lick community love using Red 03 in their bedrooms and living rooms, for a cosy feel that's brimming with personality.

TEAL 03

Our main go-to for anyone wanting to dip a toe into the dark side, but looking for something a little richer than straight-up grey: Teal 03's warmth – and mix of blue and green undertones – makes it surprisingly versatile. It's cropped up loads in bedrooms, hallways and living spaces.

GREEN 02

A community favourite thanks to its close links to nature, this soft sage green has done it all: it's been colour-drenched in bedrooms, painted onto kitchen cabinets, paired with white in traditional schemes and even adorned the walls of a houseboat renovation.

BEIGE 03

Neutral fans love this versatile light beige. It can look either contemporary or traditional depending on how it's used, it pairs like a dream with other neutrals or bolder colours, and works in both lighter and darker spaces.

GREEN 05

It's not hard to see why this warm olive green is one of our most-loved colours. Energising yet restorative, our community have embraced it in all areas of the home, including furniture upcycling projects, where it really pops as a darker accent.

PINK 07

With its calming air and earthy undertones, this mid-toned pink is often picked by those looking for an alternative to richer neutrals such as beige, and has proved popular in bedrooms, living rooms and kitchens.

BLUE 07

Blue, but make it warm. This dark, inky tone is often the top pick for those after a timeless look in their living rooms and kitchens, as it goes with pretty much everything. And despite being dark, it's far from overpowering.

PINK 01

As our unofficial 'pink for people who don't usually like pink', the super-subtle tones in Pink 01 have made it a much-loved warm neutral for those who might otherwise steer clear of this colour, but still want the warm glow that pink brings to the party.

Crack the colour code

To help you get the most out of this book – and I REALLY do want you to get interactive and engage with the exercises – I've devised a couple of different frameworks to help you.

First, the colour code – to help make it easier to understand colours (and how they work together), we've added in a few symbols as shorthand to show this visually.

Here are the basics, which you'll spot cropping up on the coming pages:

Undertones

The tones present within a colour that alter its final appearance, depending on what other colours they are mixed with.

Temperature

A colour's physical appearance (whether it looks warm or cool). This is affected by its undertones as well as the colour itself. Colours which contain both a warm and cool undertone are generally considered balanced.

Light   Mid   Dark/heavy

Weight

Whether a colour appears visually light or dark (or somewhere in the middle).

Orientation

The direction your room is facing (so north, east, south or west). This will affect the type of light it receives, and in turn how your chosen room colours look and feel.

Energising   Cosy & warm   Light & airy   Dark & moody   Calm & relaxing

Colour Psychology

The type of atmosphere you want to create. These symbols mean specific tones are used to evoke these feelings.

Six steps to your perfect palette

At the end of each chapter you'll find a specially designed activity or checklist, to help you summarise what you've learned so far and form your ideas. So by the end of this book you'll have the perfect guide to help you with any future projects.

You can complete the activities on your own sheets of paper, but to make life easier, I've also provided a QR code that links to a webpage where you can download the relevant pages as a PDF, to print out or use digitally.

To give you an overview, here's what we'll be learning:

 Play with paint: Simple colour mixing techniques; Create your own colour wheel

 Analyse: What inspires you?

 Investigate: Assess your practicalities and restrictions

 Define: Firm up your design aims

 Create: Make a physical moodboard; create a digital reference document; lay out your Lick samples by colour ratio proportions

 Summarise: Crack your own colour code

By the end of the set, you'll have everything you need to make confident, perfect-for-you decorating decisions for both your current and future projects, and a really useful resource to refer back to as a memory refresher.

The beginnings of design democratisation

While decorating our humble abodes goes back to prehistoric times, with early humans using natural pigments to decorate their cave walls, interior design as we know it has only really been a 'thing' for a century or so.

Before the 20th century, the upper classes relied on architects and talented craftspeople to create their lavish interiors (while everyone else just made do). But in the early 20th century, American actress and socialite Elsie de Wolfe pioneered the idea of interior design and decoration as a professional service. Known for her use of lighter, feminine colours and fresh, comfortable decor, she is often credited as the mother of modern interior decoration.

And in just a few generations since, design itself has had the ultimate makeover, transformed from a luxury service accessible to only the wealthiest in society to the widely accessible and affordable field it is today. Here's how that happened – and why it has shaped where things are heading:

How design became democratised

In the first half of the 20th century, the average home was modest and functional, containing a fraction of the 'stuff' we fill our houses with today. Furniture was built to last, fixed when broken, and cherished as the valuable possessions they were. But the prosperous post-war years in the 1950s caused a shift and spurred the modern DIY movement, where home improvements became a leisure activity (rather than a frugal necessity). Suddenly, interior design advice was aimed at the middle classes rather than (just) the elites, with newly launched magazines explaining HOW to renovate and decorate (or keep up with the latest trends) rather than simply showing the exquisite tastes of the wealthy. Homemaking, and impressing the neighbours with your good taste, was a hot topic.

By the 1960s, with TVs in many homes, more formal, multi-room layouts began to fall out of favour as family rooms and open-plan spaces became more practical for the modern household. The 1970s saw the rise of mass-market and flat-pack furniture, with its simple designs and shapes, and was considered contemporary and stylish, while mail-order catalogues made it easier than ever to shop from a far wider range of designs and styles without even leaving the house.

The bold, daring design styles of the 1980s sparked the craze for decorative paint effects, with households eagerly buying the latest interiors books and magazines, keen to learn how to stencil, rag roll and scumble-glaze their own homes (or just watch other people attempting it instead on TV makeover shows). This offered an early glimpse into design voyeurism – now, we could all be armchair critics or peek into other people's homes. Yet this decorating exuberance proved too much for some and as we entered the 1990s, it became common to paint out this pattern and vibrancy and replace it with grey. On everything...

Different ways of thinking

The environment and era we grow up in shapes our design perspectives, even subconsciously. Those raised in the 1950s and 1960s experienced a more prescribed design approach, following set trends and decorating to impress others, while younger generations have generally embraced more diverse, liberal influences, leading to an individualistic approach to design.

I tend to find that older clients (no judgement!) are more likely to default to traditional norms, like painting ceilings and woodwork white. Younger clients, having grown up with more freedom of self expression and a desire to use design to represent their personalities, may have fewer fixed preconceptions. Though interestingly, some trends are coming full circle: those born in the 1990s and 2000s under the shadow of climate change and spiralling living costs, are often more conscious of the financial and environmental burden of disposable decor than their parents. As a result, they're more likely to make sustainable and second-hand purchases, or upcycle existing furniture to suit their style instead of buying new – which is pretty similar to the approach their grandparents (or great-grandparents) would have taken 70 years ago.

Popular decorating colours by decade

1940s

Wartime hardship led to the popularity of muted, earthy tones like olive green, rust and brown, to represent stability and steadfastness in the face of adversity. While this palette is quite sombre and serious, it's also pretty cosy and inviting – think chilly evenings curled up by the fire with a hot cup of cocoa.

1950s

As an antidote to the previous difficult decades, joyful, sugary-sweet pastel tones became hugely popular in home design, with soft pinks, pistachio green and baby blues all synonymous with this decade. These carefree sherbert tones literally lifted the mood and introduced a fresher feel to the average home.

1960s

Fights for equality and liberation dominated this decade, with its spirit of creating new, inclusive social norms spurring the hippie movement (as well as the psychedelic movement, typified by lurid, hyper-real colours and trippy patterns). Colours were intense and saturated to match the spirit of the times.

1970s

As styles diversified further, the 1970s was heavily influenced by disco, rock and punk music across both fashion and interiors, leading to glitzy and gaudy decor styles. Earthy tones offered a counterbalance to this, although they also took on more punchy colours such as tangerine orange, avocado green and (many shades of) brown.

1980s

The 1980s was bold and brash – its general vibe and design approach was basically go hard or go home. The typical 80s palette reflected this, featuring lots of pure, bright tones and masculine colours – but when more feminine tones did come out to play, they were pretty full-on, too.

1990s

As a bit of a backlash, the typical 1990s palette was a lot more subdued, and grey interiors became a hugely popular antidote to all those primaries. Jewel tones accompanied, leaning on the cooler purple side of the spectrum (and leading many people growing up during this decade to hold a life-long aversion to lilac).

The digital design revolution

As the internet became more accessible in the early 2000s, it quickly transformed how we consumed interiors content. Initially, this was limited to 'weblogs', mainly written by design enthusiasts and hobbyists, keen to share their thoughts (accompanied by the odd pixelated image). This marked a more democratised, accessible approach to design: alongside speaking to professional interior designers and consuming traditional media, these virtual voices – from home-renovation amateurs to self-taught creators – broadened the mix, offering access that was often more direct and relatable.

The rise of Wi-Fi and mobile broadband later in the decade made accessing this content far easier, leading to new platforms like Tumblr, which favoured short-form, visual-focused posts. Its accessibility made it simpler for readers to comment, enabling two-way conversations and even friendships.

Ultimately, this paved the way for photo-sharing social media platforms like Flickr, Pinterest and Instagram, making it easier to see multiple creators' content in one feed and build a sense of community among followers. These sites let us peek into ordinary homes just like ours, see how their owners had decorated them, and learn how they went about it (rather than just a glossy 'after' shot).

The popularity of TikTok – a relatively new social sharing app – stems from this collective desire for more realistic content (posts are often less polished than Instagram's, and focus more on authenticity and creativity alongside quick, actionable DIY and design tutorials). This influence has almost come full circle, with a new breed of interiors magazines now homing in on budget-savvy, reader-led renovations (alongside designer-led projects), for a broader sense of representation.

How the pandemic reshaped life at home

In 2020, the pandemic (and subsequent lockdowns) forced us to radically re-evaluate our homes, which took on more roles than ever (whether they were geared up for it or not), from home gyms to working hubs for home-schooling kids and hot-desking adults. This shift quickly revealed the aspects in our designs or layout that didn't quite work, with some of us wishing for a few MORE walls as we navigated sharing a single living space with so many different requirements.

Unsurprisingly, this sparked a huge DIY boom, driven both by necessity and new-found free time for those who weren't working. And what was interesting is that, whether consciously or not, many of us moved towards adding a little more colour and personality to our homes, or naturally leaning on nature's colour palette as a means of creating a soothing atmosphere indoors.

Colour is so influential on our moods, and can really support our overall wellbeing, and with the rest of the world effectively closed for business, some found those grey walls – which might previously have felt soothing after a stressful day at the office – suddenly felt a bit cold and oppressive. With so much external stimulation lost, we needed our homes to replace this, and colour and pattern became the best way to go about it. By spending so much time in them we really started to understand the potential of our homes, and colour's ability to unleash it.

While virtual design services existed long before the pandemic, video calling apps like Zoom becoming mainstream allowed design experts to easily link up with clients around the world. This opened up different ways to work with an expert, from affordable design consultations helping homeowners steer their own home DIY project to fully managed design services.

It also opened the doors to a range of experts with more specialised or niche focuses, from colour consultants (hello!) to professional home de-clutterers and property stylists, enabling a greater range of people to get the look and feel they really wanted.

Insight

Tech research company Appinio conducted a survey into how social media users are interacting with interiors content: the results revealed that 69% of social media users are following home improvement project accounts (Instagram takes the lead here), with 57% emulating a DIY project they've seen on their feeds. Almost two-thirds have made DIY purchases after seeing trusted influencers or website reviews recommending specific home-improvement products, showing the impact social media has had on how we design and decorate our homes.

What's next?

Now more than ever, what we bring into our homes – and how we choose to decorate them – has become more personal, expressive and reflective (even political). Just as fashion and music are often signifiers of our broader identity, our homes (through the spotlight of social media as well as IRL visitors) now do the same.

And fortunately, some of the snobbery associated with decades past has gone, too: half a century ago, a home decorated with mismatched second-hand finds would likely have been looked down on, whereas now it's considered not only thrifty, but a commendable and sustainable way to shop. There's a great pride and sense of satisfaction to be found in personalising or upcycling these discarded treasures.

But with so much advice out there – and far more liberation when it comes to trends and design approaches – it can be daunting to know who to listen to, especially when so many voices have potentially conflicting advice or opinions.

My advice is first, take a deep breath, and second, remember there is no right or wrong. The beauty of where we are now is that you can borrow ideas from all these wonderful voices to help find your own unique path. It's not my vibe to tell people what to do (and creating your own room or home scheme from scratch is equally as valid as hiring a designer or colour consultant), but what I would advise is to make sure you're listening to a range of voices, from both experts and online communities, as that way you'll generate a far more rounded picture. The online world is changing so fast, with new opportunities emerging all the time to learn and engage, as well as smart tools like Pinterest, which allow you to collate all of this with ease. Just keep listening.

A few interesting stats

+ A recent customer survey conducted by IKEA revealed that 43% of us feel that, in a chaotic world, having a place to unwind is the number one home priority – while 33% stated the right amount of privacy at home is one of the most important things for feeling content and at ease.

+ An online article in *The Conversation* has shared that savouring fleeting moments of 'micro-joys' has been proven to benefit our wellbeing, such as drinking from a favourite mug or placing a much-loved ornament on your desk.

+ Researched published on digital library platform Wiley showed that concerns relating to ethics and sustainability are leading 63% of millennials to pay more for sustainable homeware goods.

Consumer-centred choices

Today, the ways we can access design content, advice, ideas and instructions is more pick-and-mix than linear and top-down, allowing you to find the right guidance and inspiration you need to bring your projects to life. Here's a few routes to navigating this, which you can curate to suit your confidence levels, budget or timeframe (whatever they may be):

Expert guidance (one-to-many)

+ Online interior design courses and workshops

+ Books and magazines (authored by design experts)

+ Professional amateur (self taught influencer, respected voice)

Expert guidance (one-to-one)

+ Interior designer (creates entire project)

+ Niche designer/specialist (focusing on topics like colour, organisation, styling or home staging)

+ Consultancy services – hybrid approach; advice given but consumer does the work

Consumer

+ Pinterest

+ Instagram

+ Online apps and tools to organise design ideas or create floor plans (such as Google SketchUp and Canva)

Curate (helpful tools)

+ Fellow social media users/ micro influencers

+ Social media sharing

+ Blogger/self-published author

+ Readers' homes in magazine

Peers (community/hobbyists)

Small-space living in a London studio

This studio apartment was the first home my husband and I bought together, so it'll always be close to my heart. It gave me a crash course on how to maximise every inch of a small home – a skill that's come in very handy when helping clients in cities like New York, where space is at a premium.

Due to its below-ground-level position, it lacked natural light: to balance this out we colour drenched the entire space with warm White 03 across ceilings, walls and woodwork, to blur the room's boundaries and help the space feel larger.

The rest of our colour scheme features pops of yellow, blue and green, a palette we took from the artwork above our bed, featuring Trebarwith Strand (a landmark we love in Cornwall, south-west England). To divide our sleeping area from the rest of the space without losing any precious light, we installed a Crittal-inspired glass screen – and oriented our sofas and dining area away from our sleeping space – to create a feeling of separation.

This space felt really snug and we loved living here, but when the pandemic hit – at the exact time we were launching Lick and needed more space than ever – we decided to move out of the city and into a rented home.

We all face restrictions when decorating our homes, whether that's down to money, time, or the need to keep your landlord (or partner!) happy.

I've always enjoyed making the most of wherever I've called home, whether it's somewhere I've owned or rented. Being a multiple mover has allowed me to explore and refine my style, with each relocation teaching me something new and ultimately improving my design practice along the way.

@tash_lickcolour; room colour drenched in White 03 Photo: @claramolden

@tash_lickcolour; room colour drenched in White 03 Photo: @claramolden

Escape to the country

This super-cute traditional farmer's cottage, down the road from my parents' home in Somerset, south-west England, was humble in size but gave us loads more space and light. Although we were renting, it provided a great playground to try out our new paints (luckily our landlord was very accommodating!) and put our stamp on the space.

To make it feel warm and welcoming while reflecting its rural heritage, I chose tones with earthy pigments and a touch of black to them, which felt more appropriate for an older property. I also kept all the woodwork light, painting it in warm White 03, which would have been the traditional choice rather than coloured woodwork. I then introduced brighter tones through my furniture and soft furnishings, to bring in a bit more vibrancy.

In the living room, Pink 04 on the walls created an uplifting, cosy backdrop, which became the colour I used throughout the house for a feeling of continuity. Bold, modern artworks and accessories, like the vibrant yellow vase pictured above right, introduced more playful colours and added more of our personalities to the space.

In our guest bedroom, Green 02 on the walls provided a soft and soothing backdrop, with those pink tones picked up in curtains and bedlinen. A charming green vintage chest of drawers brought in a touch of vibrancy that still sat comfortably with the rest of the space, for a harmonious feel.

But as the business took off, London called, and back to the city we went...

@tash_lickcolour; walls in Pink 04, woodwork in White 03 Photo: @emmalewisphotographer

@tash_lickcolour; walls in Green 02, woodwork in White 03 Photo: @emmalewisphotographer

Into an upside-down rented Georgian space

This property was almost the opposite of our basement studio. It had HUGE windows that filled the space with so much gorgeous light, and as its large open-plan living space was on the top floor, it felt even brighter. As this was also a rental, we had to negotiate painting the existing grotty magnolia walls with our landlord, who requested we stick with neutral colours. And actually this turned out to be the best option, as the space was just so lovely and bright, I wouldn't have wanted to use darker tones on the walls even if I'd been able to. White 06 proved the perfect option here, with its subtle pink undertones providing a hint of soothing warmth.

We evolved the yellow, green and blue palette we used in our London studio apartment by bringing in more pinks through our accessories and artwork, to reflect the pink tint in the walls and offer a contrast against the greens (which is pink's opposite colour).

This house was full of stunning Georgian features, but as it only had one bedroom – and we were starting to expand our family – we opted to move to a larger rental property to give us the space we needed to grow.

@tash_lickcolour; room colour drenched in White 06

Family life in our rented Victorian home

Our current rental is still in London, but it has a unique cottage-like vibe which I love; like a little patch of countryside in the heart of the city. Knowing it would become our family home, and with our landlord happy for us to paint freely, I embraced the chance to add a little more colour again.

Our son's nursery scheme was formed around the gorgeous painting above the fireplace as I knew we'd all be spending a lot of time in this room and I wanted it to feel joyful and inviting. As a huge art lover, this is an approach I often take, as it helps pull your whole room together (and artists know their palettes, so if you're translating similar tones into your decor, you can't really go wrong).

Then in our north-facing dining room – which doubles as a home office during the day – we added a statement wall in bold Black 02, chosen strategically to disguise an original black Gothic fireplace which isn't really my style. Now, it's far less noticeable and adds a pop of drama as you enter the room. Using earthier White 05 on the rest of the walls and ceiling helps keep the space light and softens the contrast.

While we don't own this home, we certainly feel settled here and have loved making it feel like ours as we embark on our parenthood adventures.

@tash_lickcolour; walls in Black 02 and White 05

@tash_lickcolour; walls in Yellow 02 and White 03

Working with colour

The colours we fall in love with and connect to – or those we deeply dislike but can't quite explain why – are a very personal experience. Often this is instinctive, and related to a good (or bad) memory, yet the way our eyes perceive colour and how and where we use it in our homes all plays a part in this sometimes-visceral reaction.

How colour makes us feel is always at the centre of the presentations and talks I give, but the colour wheel can be the gateway to understanding colour theory, emotional response and the science that underpins all of this. It can help to demystify why some colours are a match made in heaven while others simply look 'off' (but you can't put your finger on why).

While I want you to discover how to create a home that makes your heart sing – rather than just somewhere that looks good on the 'gram – learning these 'rules' will give you the confidence to choose when to follow or break them, as well as leading you to your perfect palette. By understanding the colour wheel, you'll be able to create colour harmonies that are cohesive and flow naturally from room to room in a way that feels right for you.

1

In this chapter, I will walk you through some of the slightly more technical aspects of colour in a way that's easy to follow, helping you to truly understand what colour is and in turn appreciate the many weird and wonderful effects it has on our minds and moods. Trust me, once you've mastered the basics, you'll be empowered to become your own colour consultant and make informed colour choices with confidence.

Introducing the colour wheel

You may have hazy recollections of learning the basics of colour mixing at school, but to refresh your memory and give a little context I want to first explain the science. And while swotting up on this when you just want help choosing the right colours for your living room might feel excessive, bear with me: once you understand the colour wheel and how to use it in interior decorating, your colour-making decisions will become infinitely easier.

The colour wheel's origin story

The colour wheel as we know it was created by the mathematician Sir Isaac Newton in the 17th century. Observing the way white light passed through a prism, he revealed how it's composed of the seven colours we see in a rainbow: red, orange, yellow, green, blue, indigo and violet.

Part of the reason Newton's findings became so widely adopted was down to the way he displayed his research as a sequential, coloured circular diagram, which clearly showed how each of these seven colours interact with and blend into each other. The standard colour wheel we use today consists of 12 colours, but otherwise still closely follows Newton's original diagram and findings, almost 400 years later.

Colour and light

It's impossible to talk about colour without also talking about light, as, essentially, colour IS light. The colours we see all around us are technically light waves, made from different wavelengths and energy, which our eyes perceive as colour. When we look at a 'green' leaf, we're actually looking at the wavelengths our eyes interpret as green reflecting from the surface of the leaf. If we also see red veins, that's because its veins are reflecting the wavelengths we interpret as red. Pretty mind-blowing, right?

The colours we see in the rainbow represent the wavelengths we can detect, which at one end starts with red (which has the longest visible wavelengths) and at the other, violet (with the shortest). The colours closest to these boundaries are harder for our eyes to read, while those that sit in the middle – yellows, greens and blues – are generally easier for us to process.

This corresponds to the way we process colour, which is via just three receptors: one for longer wavelengths (reds), one for medium wavelengths (greens) and one for shorter wavelengths (blues). Our eyes convert the combinations and strengths of these wavelengths and present them to us as the multitude of colours we can see. They even mix different wavelengths together to make colours that don't technically exist – known as non-spectral colours – such as magenta and cyan; these have no wavelengths themselves, but are the colours our eyes produce when their receptors are hit with a certain mix of both blue/red or blue/green wavelengths.

I know this is quite science-heavy, but it is really useful to understand as the length of these wavelengths affects not only what colours we see, but also how we perceive them. For instance, because red has the longest wavelength, it actually makes it feel nearer to us, so it commands our attention far more than violet, which visually recedes. This knowledge is key to making informed colour choices: the visual warmth and prominence of longer-wavelength reds and oranges can create a cosy, intimate feel, while the cooler, more distant shorter-wavelength blues and violets can feel more atmospheric and give the illusion of space.

Colour wheel overview

The colour wheel offers an easy visual way to make sense of all this theory. While most of us turn to paint charts when choosing colours for our homes, it's well worth consulting the colour wheel too, to help you understand the complex yet magical relationships to be found within colour combinations. By taking an informed approach to choosing colours, you'll be able to tailor the exact feelings and atmosphere you want to evoke, as well as creating an aesthetically pleasing look.

The basis of the standard colour wheel is the three primary colours – blue, yellow and red – which can be thought of as the 'parent' or foundational colours. The other nine colours on the wheel are essentially mixed from these three primaries. This can be broken down as follows:

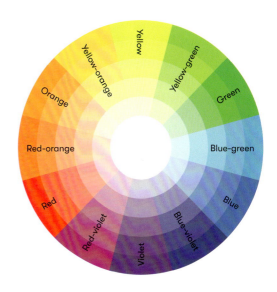

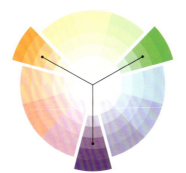

PRIMARY COLOURS

Cannot be made by mixing other colours together, and as such they are sometimes referred to as 'pure' colours. They each sit with three spaces between them on the colour wheel.

SECONDARY COLOURS

Mixed from equal quantities of two different primary colours, these can be considered easier on the eye than pure primaries. They sit in between the primary colours.

TERTIARY COLOURS

Each tertiary colour sits in between the primary and secondary colours that make it, containing an equal mix of the two. Tertiary colours fill the remaining gaps between the secondary and primary colours.

Colour wheel basics: hues and mixers

Shade (hue + black)

Tone (hue + grey)

Tint (hue + white)

Hue (pure colour)

Now let's take a more nuanced look at how the wheel works. Here we look at the colour wheel as more of a spectrum, with the addition of colour gradients along each segment. These break down into hues, tints, tones and shades: four terms that are incredibly useful to understand. Just as the three primary colours can be thought of as the parents of the other nine colours on the wheel, hues can be considered the parents of tints, tones and shades (the word 'mixers' can also be used as an umbrella term for tints, tones and shades).

All of these terms are sometimes referenced interchangeably in everyday use, but within this book we'll be sticking to the correct terminology to help you better understand the principles. Getting to grips with how these mixers alter their parent hue will give you a much clearer understanding of colour.

Hue: think of hues as the head of the household within the colour wheel. A hue is the dominant base colour within any colour family (all 12 colours that head up the colour wheel are hues). A true hue contains no black, white or grey (and these three colours aren't hues, either), which is why they are also sometimes referred to as 'pure' colours.

Tint: the addition of white paint to any hue. This will, unsurprisingly, create lighter or pastel versions of the same colour, depending on how much white is used.

Tone: add grey (in other words, a mix of black and white) to any hue and it will literally produce a 'toned down' version of that colour. This can create a more nuanced colour that bears less resemblance to its original hue compared to tints and shades, and can also be either lighter or darker (depending on how much grey is added to the original).

Shade: pure black mixed with any hue. This will both darken and dull the original colour. A little black goes a long way, and this can't be reversed by simply adding in white (instead, it'll create a grey version of the original colour).

Altering blue with mixers

Here, we've used the same blue hue as the starting point to visually demonstrate how adding different quantities of these mixers affects the colour outcomes. Generally speaking, tones and shades can create a more muted effect than tints; the former can be more sympathetic in a period property or for those looking to create a traditional, heritage aesthetic, while the latter have a cleaner, more vibrant feel, which works well in new homes or for creating a fresh look.

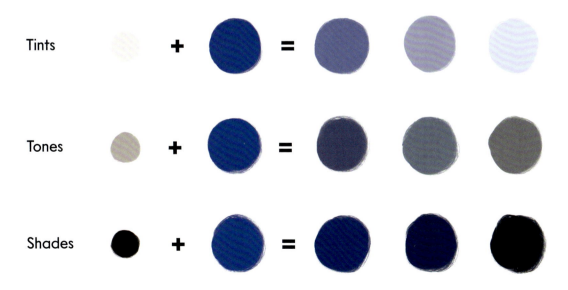

Tints

Tones

Shades

Warm and cool colours: a tale of two halves

We'll talk a lot in this book about how and when to use warm and cool colours, and it's actually quite a meaty subject; there are a number of factors to consider when choosing what's best – from the natural light levels in the room you want to decorate to the feeling you want to evoke (some of the psychology behind this will blow your mind).

But let's start simple and work our way up. At its basic level, we can neatly take the 12 hues of the colour wheel and split them down the middle, with warm reds, oranges and yellows on one side and cool greens, blues and violets on the other (see below). Even without this visual, it's pretty intuitive: warm colours (with their longer wavelengths) tend to feel energising, cosy and cheerful, while cool colours (those with shorter wavelengths) can be described as calming, tranquil and refreshing. This can give you a really useful steer when considering which way to go.

There are also colours that sit somewhere in the centre, such as the more middle-ground greens, and they can be considered more moderate in their general vibe. However, these will all still have a predominance towards warm or cool, even if it's so subtle you can barely see it.

That said, it's a common misconception to think this means that ALL colour derivatives of warm hues will therefore be warm – and equally, that any variations of cool hues will be cold. In fact, it's down to what they're mixed with, which is where overtones and undertones come into play.

In the coming pages you'll start to see symbols designed to help you understand the breakdown of different colours, such as their 'weight' (how pale or dark they look) and 'temperature' (whether they're warm or cool), alongside their undertones. These might feel a little alien at first but as we go through our colour journey, I promise it'll all make sense and really help when you start refining your perfect palette later on. You can always refer back to page 10 for an overview, if you need to refresh your memory.

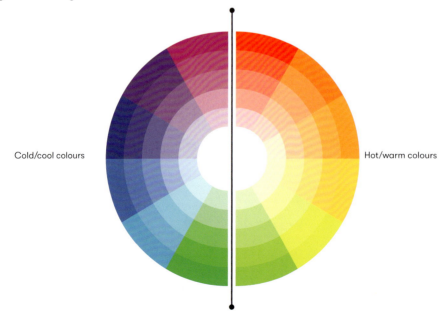

Cold/cool colours   Hot/warm colours

Undertones and overtones

Understanding overtones and undertones is key to helping you take your colour theory a step further. The clue here is in the name: think of an overtone as a colour's more obvious appearance – how you might describe that colour at first glance – while an undertone is what makes up its construction and is often far less apparent. Think of undertones almost as a secret decorating superpower: find the one that works best for your space, and you can basically decorate in whatever colour you want and be confident it'll look fabulous.

What colour is grass? It's green, right? Well, yes, but technically speaking we are looking at a green wavelength, and the type of greens we see will be impacted by whether it sits towards the yellow or blue side of the spectrum. Or, to put it into plain English, we are seeing a colour dominated by a green overtone, which (like all colours) will also have one or more undertones. So, when we think of fresh spring shoots, their more vibrant yellow undertone helps them stand out from older winter grasses, which tend to have brown or grey undertones. We notice the spring shoots as the vibrancy of their undertone draws our attention more sharply.

Usually overtones (sometimes called the 'mass tone') are quite straightforward to spot, unless they fall neatly between two hues (such as teal, which is usually a fairly even mix of blue and green and the overtone can be a little harder to identify). But undertones provide the secret sauce when it comes to making your favourite colours tie in perfectly with your preferred palette. Every colour has one or more undertones (aside from the three primary hues of pure red, blue and yellow, plus pure white and pure black): get them right, and they'll become your new decorating best friend.

Crack the colour code: breaking down three greens

By viewing three Lick paint swatches broken down by their undertones, temperature and weight, can you see how these elements have impacted the look and feel of their final overtone?

Paint colour	Undertones	Temperature	Colour weight	
GREEN 02				The combination of both blue and grey undertones in Green 02 gives it a soft sage look, resulting in a colour that's understated and easy to live with.
GREEN 09				Calming Green 09's delicate tone gives it a cool yet clear look, reminiscent of thin, wispy summer stems dancing in a meadow.
GREEN 05				Incorporating a single undertone, you probably don't need a symbol to tell you it's yellow that gives Green 05 its energising, olive glow and uplifting, feel-good vibe.

The basics: monochromatic (tonal)

Did you know that the term monochrome – or monochromatic – doesn't just mean black and white? This is often misunderstood, but it actually refers to any colour scheme which uses just one colour that's lightened (tinted) with white or darkened (shaded) with black. For example, a monochromatic blue scheme could consist of a dark navy, going right up to a pale duck egg, all from one base hue.

These schemes are often referred to as tonal, and can give a harmonious, visually cohesive look. On the plus side, this can result in a room that feels relaxing and considered, but – dare I say it – if you play it super-safe it could run the risk of just feeling a little boring. Technically speaking it can be quite hard to create a completely monochromatic room, so this is often used as shorthand for a space that features a monochromatic paint colour palette, but perhaps brings in a little contrast with accessories or art.

If I'm working with a client who is particularly colour-cautious, I'll often start them with a tonal scheme as it's a great way to help them slowly introduce colour into their homes (and you kind of can't go wrong, as a tonal palette is naturally quite restrictive). I also love how schemes like this can help make a small room feel bigger.

Photo: @_richardkiely; walls in Beige 03, units Beige 02

Choosing a monochromatic palette: Richard's kitchen

To add warmth and interest to a neutral scheme... take your cue from this sleek kitchen, which follows a cosy neutral pathway from white (on the kitchen worktops) all the way to black (on its accents).

Technically, this scheme is more achromatic (which refers to schemes 'without colour', aka greyscale), as – although its palette is monochromatic – it doesn't directly correspond to any of the 12 colour wheel segments. But in interior design, the term 'achromatic' is often used to refer to warmer 'near'-neutrals (because who actually lives in a completely colourless box?!). So here, the journey from white to black follows a softer, beiges-and-browns monochromatic route instead.

Choosing a monochromatic palette: Athena's bedroom

To make it more maximal... push the tonality of reds and pinks to the max, like this bedroom, which uses a warm, cocooning pink on both walls and curtains and a paler taupe tone on flooring and furniture. Rather than painting the sloping ceiling in a pure white, which would feel jarring, this warmer off-white fits in more effortlessly while helping the space feel larger. Pops of red in the bed linen add a jolt of interest without being overstimulating for a sleeping space.

@topologyinteriors; walls in Pink 03 Photo: @chriswhartonphotography

The basics: analogous

Analogous colours, which are also sometimes referred to as adjacent, are the shades, tints and tones that sit next to each other on the colour wheel. If you look at any one segment of the wheel, that segment plus the two either side of it would together make an analogous palette.

This closeness means the range of colours to choose from within an analogous scheme isn't too broad, resulting in combinations that are easy on the eye and instantly compatible. You often find this blend of analogous palettes in nature, making these groupings feel soothing and peaceful.

@thishovehome; room colour drenched in White 06

Going for a walk in the countryside demonstrates analogous colours 'in action'. Think of how the green fields sit against the blue sky, and how this effect is amplified on a sunny summer's day, while in winter the colours and contrasts become a lot more muted.

Choosing an analogous palette: Lucinda's hallway

To give a nod to nature… bring in all those lovely blue and green tones we associate with the great outdoors. I love how Lucinda's hallway is a little sneaky here, with a warm neutral used over everything, but then you have this almost jarring jolt from the gorgeous green statement artwork, and a lovely pop of deep blue on the walls of the room leading off. I say almost jarring because, actually, the warm neutral paint in this space has a yellow undertone, and the artwork also contains yellow tones, helping it all sit together harmoniously.

Choosing an analogous palette: Mary's bedroom

To bring in bolder accents...
go for more unexpected colour choices in areas that aren't directly in your eyeline, allowing you to introduce fairly punchy colours without them feeling overbearing. Here, Mary's bedroom keeps this vibrant warm purple tone restricted to the floors, and uses an equally bold blue on her bedside table, while the walls are a far gentler blue-green shade.

@marycharteris: walls in Blue 01
Photo: @jon_aaron_green_photographer

The basics: complementary

Complementary colours are perfect for when you want to bring in a little drama but also need assurance it'll look awesome in the flesh. This scheme is sometimes referred to as contrasting, but because the colours live directly opposite each other on the wheel they are still easy on – and appealing to – the eye. By their nature, complementary pairings will always contain one warm and one cool colour segment, which brings in a little more visual friction and interest.

There can be a lot of outdated stigmas around opposite colours, with the well-known phrase 'red and green should never be seen' essentially referring to complementary colours. But by simply dialling down the intensity you can find a far less shouty combination, like the two seen here, which can be easier to live with. Working your way up and down these opposite segments, however you choose to pair them, will always yield fabulous results.

When we think of sunsets, we often imagine that warm golden light as the sun goes down. But if you're lucky you might also see one of those glorious pink twilight skies. Green and pink schemes like those shown here are reminiscent of this, with darker greens representing the trees deepening in colour as night falls.

Choosing a complementary palette:

Katie and Byron's kitchen

To balance one strong tone... use a much lighter tint as its complementary opposite, creating a look that lets this stronger colour lead (whether it's dark or bright), while retaining a sense of balance. Here, this vibrant hunter green steals the show on these kitchen cabinets (echoed in the accessories and artwork), with this soft, subtle complementary pink on the walls acting as a warm neutral.

Katie and Byron's sitting room

To keep pinks feeling sophisticated... ground them with neutral tones and their contrasting companion: green. While this statement artwork on the end wall certainly doesn't blend into the background, it looks super cool thanks to the scale, and the herons in the artwork chime perfectly with the sofa beneath. By introducing several more subtle pinks in accent spots, and referencing the green kitchen cabinets with similarly toned fabric details in the seating area, the whole space feels unified and grown-up.

Delving deeper: double and split complementary

Now we've covered the basics of colour theory, it's time to get a little more experimental! Building on the standard complementary scheme, arrangements that are either split complementary (which use three colours) or double complementary (which use four, in two different formations) follow the same 'opposites attract' principles, while taking things up a notch. As before, you can play with the tints, tones and shades of each colour to dial the drama up or down.

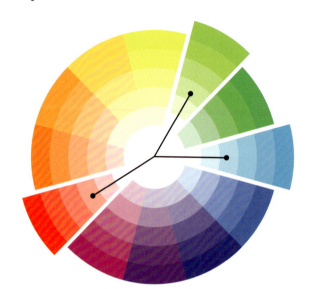

Split complementary

A split-complementary scheme brings in an extra twist: rather than choosing two direct opposites, you can deviate and use the two colours either side of the opposite colour instead, resulting in a three-colour scheme. This can provide a strong contrast when all three are used, while avoiding direct colour clashes, producing a look that's playful but not overwhelming.

A split-complementary scheme to try

For a timeless vintage vibe... pair a retro-inspired tangy green with a cool mid-toned blue and an earthy orange to form your three split-complementary colours. By choosing softened tones and shades, bringing these colours together in a scheme will create a laid-back cool vibe (rather than feeling like a retro throwback). Introducing a couple of lighter neutrals, like a soft sage and a warm, grounding pink, can help build this palette out and give you a little more to play with.

PINK 02

ORANGE 02

GREEN 07

BLUE 03

BLUE 04

Double complementary

A double-complementary scheme, usually referred to as tetradic, is frankly best reserved for maximalists, as it has a 'go big or go home' vibe. Comprising two sets of complementary colour pairings, it's considered to offer the richest overall palette combinations, regardless of which pairs you pick.

It's best explained by visualising the colour wheel with either a square or rectangle drawn on top, its corners representing your colour choices (both ways count as tetradic). With the square method, your four colours will each be three segments apart: the colour wheel here shows red-violet (aka pink), orange, yellow-green and blue. Using the rectangle method would mean picking two pairs of colours which sit one segment apart and have three spaces between each pair: e.g. if your first pair was blue and violet, your second pair would be orange and yellow.

It's important to use all four colours in different quantities within a tetradic scheme, letting one dominate while the rest play smaller roles, otherwise the final scheme will look unbalanced. But get this right and it really can look spectacular.

Choosing a double-complementary palette: Katie's son's room

For a fun, youthful feel... Katie chose to bring a lively and invigorating palette into her child's bedroom, while wisely using a calming, knocked-back blue-green tone on the bulk of the walls and ceiling to bring a more restful look when lying in bed. Note that the red and yellow tones used here aren't pure primaries; they've both been knocked back with the addition of orange to make them easier on the eye while still feeling vibrant.

@aflickofpaint; walls painted in Yellow 02 and Blue 01

Delving deeper: dyadic and triadic

Dyadic

Dyadic schemes consist of just two colours that live one apart from each other on the colour wheel. These keep your palette tight and cohesive, but by playing a little fast and loose and working up and down the various tints, tones and shades you can still create an interesting end result. Sticking with two hues from the same temperature side of the colour wheel, such as warm yellows and oranges or cool greens and blues, will provide a harmonious look. To add a little more intrigue, choose one from each side (such as, red and violet, or magenta (violet-red) and coral (red-orange).

Two dyadic schemes to try

For a cool yet intriguing mix... here, I've chosen two purple colours to represent the violet segment of the colour wheel, alongside one blue option. Purple 06 is a gorgeous pale lilac with warm pink undertones, which sits comfortably alongside its sumptuous, darker relation, Purple 03. Bring in some Blue 05, with its more vibrant hue and lilac undertones, and you've got a sophisticated yet sleek palette to work with.

For a warm, sunny scheme... borrowing from the orange and yellow segments of the colour wheel, these two colours combined can feel really uplifting, but they can still be relaxing despite their vibrancy. The intensity of red-toned Orange 01 is tempered by the more mellow brown and grey tones in Orange 03, which makes for a great dark neutral. With yellow, you could play it more tonal with an earthier orange shade, or bring in a little more friction with this pure, warm white-yellow for a cheery colour pop.

Triadic

Triadic schemes, as you might have guessed from the title, consist of three colours which are evenly spaced around the colour wheel. In practice, this means each of the three chosen colours will have three spaces between them on the wheel (so every fourth colour would form the triadic palette). The primaries red, yellow and blue form a triadic colour scheme (although I definitely wouldn't use all three in their pure forms to create a scheme as it would be way too overpowering, but variations of their tints and tones can work wonderfully).

Choosing a triadic palette: Victoria's living room

For a sophisticated, energising space... follow Victoria's lead and play with 'off' versions of the three primary colours. Here, the tones of deep red used in her sofa (and the softer mauve in the wall art) both come from the red-violet segment of the colour wheel, making them cooler and slightly more blue-toned than those found in the red segment. Her choice of wall colour and co-ordinating cushions again sits on the blue/green cusp rather than firmly within the blue segment. Tones of orange-yellow appear in other accents, while the wood trim on the glass coffee table also fits into this category.

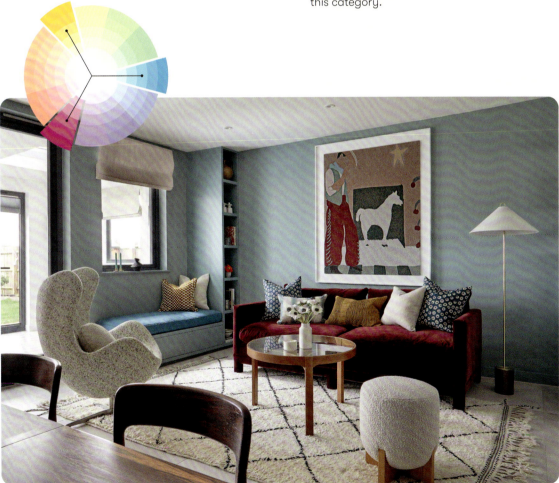

@victoria_covell_interiors; walls in Teal 01 Photo: Anna Stathaki

Become an undertone detective

Hopefully you've now got a clear understanding of the impact undertones have on your decorating decisions, and why this is so useful for making informed colour choices at home.

Though cracking the undertone code isn't an exact science – and some might be easier to spot than others – there are basic rules you can follow to help figure this out (at Lick, we always list which undertones we've added into our paints, so that's one less thing for customers to decipher). There will of course be many other elements besides paint to bear in mind when creating a scheme, and the same advice applies whether it's fabrics, furniture, floorboards or any other materials you're trying to investigate.

The best way to figure this all out is, luckily, the simplest (it's also the method we use at Lick). To successfully undertone-detect, you need to view your colour (or mixed-colour pattern) in isolation, by placing it on top or in front of a pure white background. By removing all other influences, you'll be able to see far more clearly what direction a colour seems to be leaning towards, even if it's a pale off-white rather than a bright tone.

Delving deeper

+ If you're looking at your sample against pure white and still aren't sure what you're seeing, ask yourself if it looks a little more vibrant on this background compared to any similar tones you're testing: if it does, it probably has a warm undertone like red, orange or yellow.

+ The same applies in reverse for cooler colours: if it doesn't feel like it's jumping out, it's more likely to be a cool colour with grey, blue or purple undertones. If in doubt, pick up two samples you already know are both warm and cool, of the same parent hue (say, green) so you can see how they differ against the white and each other.

+ To narrow things down further, you could also place samples against other pure primary and secondary colours to see if your warm sample seems to have more in common with red, yellow or orange, or your cool sample sits more comfortably against blue, green or purple.

Photo: @edwardconder

Place your samples here

You can use a sheet of pure white printer
paper for this, but to make things easier I've
left this page blank so you can bookmark it
and use this as your testing ground.

1

Play with paint: simple colour mixing techniques

When I'm hosting workshops or teaching online, one thing I love to do is encourage my students to get a little hands-on and play around with colour mixing to help bring the theory to life. You probably did this at school, and while you're not likely to ever actually mix your own bespoke paints for your walls or woodwork, it's an incredibly useful exercise to help hone your new undertone-spotting skills. And who doesn't love an excuse to get a little bit messy?

You'll still get the gist just from looking at the exercises on these next few pages, though if you can I really encourage you to grab some paint so you get the full picture. Ready to play?

YOU WILL NEED

Artist's paints: I recommend acrylics (you can buy small tubes relatively cheaply), but children's poster paint will do the job. Watercolours can also work, but it might be harder to see the depths of colours. Stock up on:

+ Primary red
+ Primary yellow
+ Primary blue
+ Pure white
+ Pure black

A few artist's brushes (they needn't be fancy)

Pot for water

Palette: just a surface you can dollop some paint on, such as an old cupcake tray, leftover jam jar lids or a plastic plate – whatever's to hand

Sheets of white paper, A4 or bigger

The colours of commercial household paints like Lick's are essentially mixed using these same principles (though there's a lot more to it, which we'll talk about later). If you've ever purchased paint that's mixed in-store, you might have seen this process in action, as the mixing machine adds carefully calibrated shots of colour to a base paint (usually white or black) before mixing it all together to perfectly match your colour card or paint reference in order to produce the exact tone.

Making simple tints, tones and shades

Take one blob of blue and one of white and play with using different amounts of each to see what effect this has. Repeat with a fresh blob of blue and different quantities of black (you'll notice a little goes a long way). Then, with a third blue blob, try combining it with different amounts of both white and black (aka grey, but you can just mix all three together for the same outcome, you don't have to pre-mix the grey). Repeat the same exercises with yellow and red to see how it works across all three primaries.

Tint

Tone

Shade

2

Creating secondary colours

Mix an equal amount of red and yellow to make orange and have a go at painting it onto your paper. Repeat with red and blue to make violet (aka purple), and with blue and yellow to make green.

Save back a generous blob of each as you go, to use in the next exercise.

3

Creating tertiary colours

Use your primary colours with the secondary colours you mixed and saved back in the previous exercise to create the six tertiary colours that form the remainder of the colour wheel.

Remember, tertiary colours are an equal mix of the primary and secondary colours they sit in between. So yellow (primary) and orange (secondary) makes yellow-orange. Repeat this principle to create the remaining five tertiaries: red-orange, yellow-green, blue-green, blue-violet and red-violet.

4

Creating brown

Unlike the 12 hues of the colour wheel, brown (which isn't on the wheel) is created by mixing all three primaries together.

A combination of all three – using the same amounts of red and blue but twice as much yellow – will create a 'parent' brown. You can then play with altering its tints, tones and shades through adding different amounts of white, black and grey.

5

Let loose with some freestyle mixing!

No rules here – you've created a great little set of colours, which will form the basis of this next exercise. But if you're having fun, why not carry on mixing to see what you can create? Even if you don't like the outcomes, they will help you to understand colour composition in a little more depth.

If you're feeling stuck, try the following:

+ Mix two complementary (opposite) hues together to produce a range of desaturated earthy tones and rich off-blacks.

+ Create more nuanced shades by using dark blue or dark red instead of pure black to darken them.

+ Play a bit more with brown: add some extra blue to its mix to bring out some soft purple tones, or add more red to white-tinted browns for a peachy effect.

Play with paint: create your own colour wheel

Now we've explored why the colour wheel is such an invaluable tool for the home decorator, why not make your own? While you can of course simply refer to the colour wheel visuals within this book – or purchase a pre-made one online – painting your own is a really helpful (and super-fun!) way to see the reality of the theory.

If you scan the QR code on this page, you'll be able to download and print a larger version of this blank template, or just go freehand and draw it out yourself directly on to some white paper or card.

You won't need anything in addition to the paints and supplies you used for your exercises earlier – and in fact, creating a colour wheel will help put all of that playtime into context.

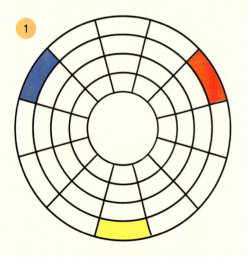

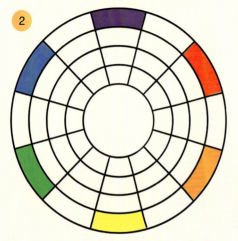

Before you start: create your wheel

Print out your colour wheel blank template (I'd recommend printing this A4) or if you're DIY'ing it, draw round a large dinner plate onto some scrap paper (the underside of wallpaper offcuts are great for this). You could use a compass to create the smaller inner circles, or just sketch them in (it's really not about perfection).

Paint in your primaries

Now, pour out a generous dollop of your three primary colours and keep these handy for mixing the rest of your colours as we go. Add your three primary colours into the outer segments.

Add in your secondaries

Just like the exercises on pages 42–45, next you'll need to mix up your three secondaries and fill these in. Use equal amounts of red and yellow to create orange, equal yellow and blue for green, and equal blue and red to make violet.

Complete the outline with tertiaries

Fill in the remaining outer segment gaps –
remember, the six remaining tertiary colours are an
even mix of their nearest primary and secondary
colours. At this stage, it'll be more obvious which two
colours to use to fill them with (so, the blank space
between red and orange will be filled with an equal
mix of red and orange, and so on).

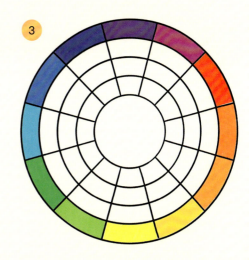

Fill in your first segment

Now you've got your basic wheel set up, it's time to
start painting the relevant tints, tones and shades in
each segment, under the 12 outer hues! Here's how it
works (starting with red).

+ Take some red and mix in a little black, to create
a shade (just use a small amount here). Paint this in
the box underneath the primary red.

+ Repeat the process, but with grey (you can use
a 50/50 mix of black and white paint to make this,
and set it aside). This will create a tone of red. Add
this to the box underneath your red shade.

+ Mix an equal amount of white with red, to create
a red tint. This will go in your final box, nearest the
centre of the wheel.

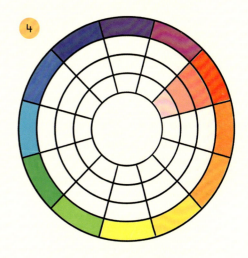

Repeat across the remaining segments

Each of the 12 colours will follow the exact same
process, and it's up to you what order you complete
them in. But to avoid smudging, you might want to
follow the same order as steps 1-3 to fill in all your
segments, painting the tints, tones and shades of
the remaining two primary colours before moving
onto the secondary then tertiary segments.

You could also create a few more specific
colour wheels, too – such as one where you use
increasingly lighter tints along each segment, or
the same with tones and shades.

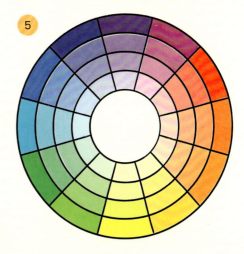

Nick and Ant's calming and elegant period home

It's fair to say that Nick and Ant's house definitely qualified as a 'doer-upper' when they first bought it. Previously uninhabited for a decade, riddled with damp and in need of total renovation, the fact they transformed it into something SO chic in only a year is testament to their hard work and dedication. The couple already had quite extensive experience in renovating North American properties, though none of this quite prepared them for the challenges this very different British house threw at them. Luckily, their keenness to learn new skills (and willingness to muck in – often quite literally) allowed them to push their budget without sacrificing their vision.

This was put to the test quite early on, when it became clear that there was far more structural damage than they'd previously thought, meaning much of the property needed stripping back to its bare bones and effectively rebuilding. But despite this major setback, they took this as an opportunity to create their dream layout from scratch, redesigning it to suit their needs perfectly. As a result, their finished home is now unrecognisable, while still totally in-keeping with the original character of this 125-year-old house.

After such an intense renovation period, their choice of refreshing White 03 to set the tone as soon as you open the front door – colour drenched across the hallway and stairs – opens up the space, while leaving the bannisters in their original wood finish shows how they've blended the home's original features with more modern decor throughout. This colour continues into their kitchen (visible from the hallway), acting as a slick backdrop for their statement marble worktop and splashback, which they've let steal the show (while also keeping other elements of the space quite simple and minimal).

WHO LIVES HERE?

Married couple Nick and Ant, both digital content creators who also co-host a podcast @oldgaysnewgays

INSTAGRAM

@studiototeda

THE PROPERTY

A three-story, Victorian mid-terrace house. On the ground floor, the main reception room leads directly off the hallway at the front of the property, while the rest of the semi-open-plan layout houses a downstairs cloakroom, kitchen and dining room which both lead onto the courtyard garden. Upstairs is the couple's bedroom, with en suite bathroom and a combined walk-in closet and laundry room, with a separate guest bedroom and bathroom further down the corridor. A previously converted attic room is now used as a bonus living and study space.

PREFERRED COLOURS AND STYLES

Scandinavian-modern with a hint of Victorian charm to reflect the history of their period home. Their pared-back palette is elevated with luxe materials like marble and glass, yet grounded with characterful vintage accents.

From the start they were keen to retain the separate rooms which are traditional in Victorian layouts, while wanting the overall layout to feel accessible. To help achieve this, rather than reinstate internal doors downstairs, they installed open archways instead, aiding a sense of flow and connection between each space. Painting the dining room in Blue 03, with its warm green undertones, helps retain this sense of separate identity while still feeling light and uplifting.

Upstairs, the original layout consisted of three bedrooms and a bathroom, which they had planned to retain. But after seeing the whole floor stripped to its shell, they decided to combine the front and middle bedrooms to create their dream suite, assigning the front room as their sleeping space, then splitting the middle room in half, adding a new door to connect the two rooms. This former bedroom now contains an en suite on one side, and a walk-in closet space on the other. Unusually for the UK, the closet also houses their washing machine (Nick is from Canada, where laundry facilities are commonly housed upstairs – he convinced Ant to install it here, rather than the kitchen). While the en suite was kept light and bright in White 03, the couple decided to play up on the comparative lack of natural light in the closet, instead colour drenching the space in earthy, rich Orange 02 as a way of embracing this darker feel.

This reconfiguration allowed them to create a clutter-free, tranquil vibe in their main sleeping area, which also incorporates a small reading nook in one corner (and has quickly become Nick's favourite spot to sit and unwind). Here, they opted for Greige

02 across all four walls (keeping woodwork and ceilings to a traditional white), chosen as the pair felt this gentle, relaxing green-toned beige really helps them unwind at the end of the day.

Their en suite exemplifies their approach of mixing traditional touches with their Scandi aesthetic – by opting for linen-style shower curtains and natural wood cabinetry, the look feels connected to its Victorian past, while sleek lines and contemporary hardware bring it bang up to date.

Nick & Ant's core house palette

KEY PARENT COLOURS

LEADING LICK PAINT PICKS

GREIGE 02   BLUE 03   WHITE 03   ORANGE 02   GREY 08

'Lick's thoughtfully curated palette really helped us find the right colours to turn the vision for our home into reality, reflecting both our styles and personalities. The calming, lighter tones we've chosen definitely give us the nurturing, chilled vibes we were after.

However, we're really glad we chose the more energising Orange 02 in our walk-in closet space – while it's very different to our main colour choices elsewhere, it still echoes other orange accents that crop up around the house, such as our bedroom pendant light and our choice of warm-toned woods across furniture and flooring.'

-ANT AND NICK-

An introduction to colour psychology

Have you ever thought about how many choices you make throughout the day that are based on colour? While some are conscious – like choosing which shoes to pair with your outfit – others are almost reflexive (if you're picking out fruit at the grocery store, you likely won't think twice about whether to select the vibrant red apple versus the one with browning skin). Colour can also become a shorthand: if you use the tube, subway or metro to get to work, you'll scan for your line on the map based on its colour rather than title.

Put simply, colour is a communicator that we use as a visual language, whether we're conveying a message to others (think of the 'serious' black business suit), or a message is being conveyed to us (that brown apple was telling you it's past its best). Colour is purposely chosen by brands to signal their personality and entice us to buy their wares: see Coca Cola, which uses its distinctive red to suggest happiness and friendship, reflecting its core values of sharing and socialising with – of course – an ice-cold Coke in hand. Utilising one of the most visually striking colours, Coke also commands our attention when we see it stacked on supermarket shelves or emblazoned on billboards.

2

Colour acts as a visual shorthand to convey a certain mood or emotion: ever noticed how high-stakes dramatic film scenes are often set against grey clouds and driving rain, while the happy-ever-afters have a backdrop of blue skies and sunshine?

These are all things we instinctively know, but how often do we ever really think about them? In this chapter, I'll help you get to grips with colour psychology and show you practical ways you can use it – whatever your colour choices – to help transform your home into a supportive haven that's unique to your individual needs.

The emotions of colour

If I could ask my clients only one question during our consultations, rather than 'what colours do you like (or dislike)?' I would ask, 'how do you want the colours in your home to make you feel?' Because colour is key to this – colour IS emotion. That might sound a bit out there, but it all comes back to the science we discussed in chapter one. But how can we learn the language, and discover how to read and speak colour? By the end of this chapter, you'll be equipped with some of these answers.

In a nutshell, colour is light and energy, and its wavelength and intensity directly impact how we perceive it – while colour psychology impacts our emotions, feelings and overall well-being.

How this happens is rooted back in science: the three types of cone receptors in our eyes (which detect red, green and blue wavelengths) are what allow us to perceive colours – but this is just the start of their journey. Once this light is detected by the cones, our brain's visual cortex translates this information into what we ultimately see, while the hypothalamus (which is like the brain's sorting depot) helps regulate our physiological and emotional responses to this stimuli, relaying this to our nervous system and triggering the release of certain hormones.

So for example, if you feel more alert staring at a red feature wall, it's because red's wavelengths can stimulate your nervous system, causing your adrenaline to rise and your heart rate to increase (and could leave you feeling on edge). But stare at a blue wall and its wavelengths can actually lower your heart rate, in turn helping you feel relaxed.

The physiology of colour isn't the whole story, though. Our personal and cultural associations also play a large part in how we perceive colours, as a whole or specific tones and shades. These can trigger instinctive reactions based on perceptions or memories (conscious or otherwise): just as a certain song can magically transport us back to that brilliant beach party (or first broken heart), colour can do the same. Regardless of its properties, you might love sunny yellow because it reminds you of happy childhoods picking buttercups in your granny's garden, or you might have a negative association with that particular shade as it evokes a bad memory.

Lifestyle is also a huge factor in choosing the colours that will best support us emotionally at home. If you're an introvert who spends your working day interacting with others outside of the house, your home might need to provide quiet respite, giving you space to wind down after a day of people-ing. But if you're more of a high-energy extrovert, you may want your home to provide a little extra stimulation, in line with your own energy levels.

Be honest with yourself: if you tend to play it safe and stick to neutral tones, is that because it's genuinely what makes you happy? Or is it because you're nervous to try something bolder – or worried what your friends might think? You might have heard the phrase, 'dance like no one's watching'; if you could DECORATE like no one's watching, would you make different choices?

This is why I'm a huge advocate of choosing colours that support how YOU want to feel, rather than trying to impress or influence others. This is extra important when it comes to the colours you decorate your own home with, as it's usually the space we spend the most time in. Who cares what someone on Instagram or a visiting relative think – they're not the ones living in it!

Psychology of the colour wheel

I said that colour was emotion, and this version of the colour wheel is one I always like to share when discussing this, as it's a great way to help understand the concept. While these are of course broad statements, and these colours won't evoke the exact same emotions in everyone, it gives you a good at-a-glance guide. Over the coming pages we'll delve into the personality of each of these colours in more detail, but this will give you a basic understanding for now.

Crack the colour code: colour combinations to spark emotion

Whether I'm designing individual paint colours for Lick, or curating a colour palette collection, these are always inspired by the moods and emotions I want them to evoke. And I've found these often fall into five core moods, shown below as symbols (which are part of the Colour Code on page 10).

In this chapter, you'll see these symbols against certain colours. Later in the book I'll also apply them to entire palettes to show you how to lead your decorating schemes by emotion – so keep an eye out for them!

Light & Airy

Energising

Cosy & Warm

Calm & Relaxing

Colour Psychology
(parent symbol)

Dark & moody

Meet the four psychological primaries

While all colours have their own unique personalities – which we perceive through the lens of our own unique personalities – four of these colours (red, yellow, blue and green) form what's known as the 'psychological colour primaries'. Understanding these can be super helpful in demystifying our complex relationships with colour.

As a rule, our brains process and react to these colours on a deep, emotional level. The four colours each trigger a different response within us, but they'll all either soothe or stimulate, depending on their intensity.

	Represents	Emotional responses
BLUE	Intellect	Affects the mind, either provoking thought or helping us feel serene.
RED	Physicality	Affects the body, either triggering our physical fight-or-flight response or helping us feel comforted.
YELLOW	The nervous system	Affects our mental state, either firing up our confidence and optimism or helping us feel relaxed and contented.
GREEN	Balance	Affects – and helps balance – our mind, body and emotions; can help us feel invigorated and uplifted, or rested and calm.

Stimulating or soothing?

Whether each of these colours falls on the stimulating or soothing side is mainly based on its saturation levels, which can be explained as follows:

+ **High saturation:** colours will appear vivid, bold, vibrant and intense. Their hue will be more dominant, meaning it's easy to see what the overtone is (for example, cobalt or navy – both highly saturated colours – are clearly blue).

+ **Low saturation:** colours will look muted or washed-out. It will be less obvious what their dominant hue is (for example, a low saturation duck egg blue usually contains a large amount of grey as well as green undertones, so visually it's less obviously blue compared to cobalt and navy).

+ **If in doubt:** if a colour seems to be shouting for attention – or it feels bold and energetic – it probably has a high level of saturation, and will therefore be more stimulating. Whereas if it feels like it's just hanging out calmly in the background, it's probably low saturation, and will have soothing properties.

Generally speaking, dark colours tend to be high saturation and light colours are usually low saturation, but that's not a hard-and-fast rule. Mid-toned colours can be either high or low saturation (like magenta – which isn't dark but is highly saturated – compared to a dusky rose, which might share a similar level of mid-tone but has a much lower saturation).

Let's get intense (or chill out)

To put into context how this relates to different paint colours, here's how it works:

BLUE		GREEN		RED		YELLOW	
BLUE 01	BLUE 07	GREEN 09	GREEN 07	PINK 01	RED 02	YELLOW 01	YELLOW 03
Mentally soothing	Mentally stimulating	Gently soothing	Gently stimulating	Physically soothing	Physically stimulating	Emotionally soothing	Emotionally stimulating

You might be surprised at just how many different moods and emotions can be created simply by tweaking the composition of these four colours. This is why I always encourage people to keep an open mind when it comes to choosing colours, and not dismiss entire spectrums with sweeping statements such as, 'I don't like blue'. By working your way through this chapter and trying out the Perfect Palette exercise on pages 82–83, you'll be able to pinpoint the exact tones of a colour you don't like – and why that is – so you can open the door to its other wonderful variations.

Remember that what we find calming or stimulating is affected by our personal preferences as well as the psychological profiles of each colour. It could be that we find calm in a room drenched with a (technically highly stimulating) dark inky blue, or mentally uplifted by a low-saturation, soothing green. Some of us thrive in a visually stimulating home, full of highly saturated colours and clashing patterns, while others would find it migraine-inducing. But equally, a serene, low-saturation space could make busy-brained individuals feel anxious, leaving little to distract them from their whirring thoughts.

Deep dive: red

COLOUR TYPE

Primary colour; psychological primary

KEY ATTRIBUTES

Stimulating, passionate, powerful, confident and warm. Red will raise your energy levels (whether you want it to or not).

IDEAL FOR

A dark hallway that lacks natural light: choosing earthier reds will give a warm and welcoming entrance.

Red sits at the start of the rainbow and has the longest wavelength our eyes can see, meaning that although it's not the easiest colour for us to read, it draws focus by visually shouting at us, commanding attention. This is why it's often associated with warnings and danger (on traffic lights, it's basically yelling, 'WHOA THERE', compared to green's gentle 'Okay, off you go' vibe).

If red were a person, you might describe it in a somewhat extreme way: at best adventurous, fun and pretty damn sexy – but at worst angry, overbearing and impatient.

Despite – or perhaps because of – this, it's still a popular colour when it comes to decorating (we've clocked that the Lick community are increasingly using it to paint whole rooms, rather than just restricting it to key feature areas). As a rule of thumb, the more shouty the red, the better it is to stick with accent-use only. But if you do want to use a highly saturated red on a larger scale, temper it by choosing a tone with black or brown pigments: this will still feel stimulating, but appear a little darker and less overbearing.

Three personalities of red

Lick's pick	Mood	How it works
RED 02		The high saturation of this dark poppy-red has a definite warmth from its yellow undertones. Adding it to a decorating scheme will bring an invigorating, energetic feeling.
RED 06		The addition of grey and purple undertones reduces the intensity of this plummy red, although it would still sit on the stimulating side when it comes to saturation. This means the energy it brings to a room is a little more subtle.
RED 03		This deep, dusky red straddles the saturation see-saw. Its warm pink and brown undertones create a more knocked-back red, which is both mentally grounding and physically stimulating, resulting in a lightly energising feel overall.

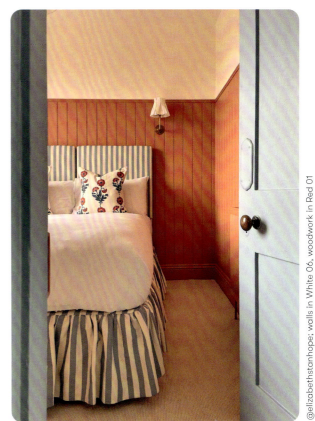

Deep dive: orange

COLOUR TYPE

Secondary colour

KEY ATTRIBUTES

Playful, energetic, fun, welcoming and enthusiastic. Orange can feel like an old friend opening the door and inviting you in for a long overdue catch-up.

IDEAL FOR

Kitchen or dining rooms (orange both fosters conversation and stimulates the appetite). It's often used in meeting rooms to encourage creativity and open-ness (the same principles could be applied to a cosy Zooming corner at home).

Made from equal parts red and yellow, it's no surprise that orange sits firmly on the warm side of the colour wheel. Offering less intensity than red, while feeling somewhat mellower than pure yellow, you probably don't need me to tell you that it can induce feelings of warmth, friendliness and positive energy. It can even look a little bit magical: think of that glorious 'golden hour' glow leading up to sunset – there's a reason why many wedding photographers (and influencers) like to shoot portraits at this time of day. It can help us – both literally and metaphorically – look on the bright side of life.

But orange can sometimes get a bit of a bad rap, with the more garish mixes appearing cheap and cheerful. It also fell out of favour after its heyday in the 1970s, partly because household lighting transitioned from warm tungsten filament bulbs – which had emphasised its cosiness – to brighter, cooler LED alternatives, which instantly made it look overpowering. Thankfully, today's LED bulbs are available in the warmer tones of the tungsten heyday, which might have helped the resurgence of retro colours and styles in recent years.

Three personalities of orange

Lick's pick	Mood	How it works
ORANGE 01		This dark blood orange looks obviously stimulating. Its warm red undertones influence this, and the combination of warm orange and fiery red makes for an energising tone that could work well in creative settings.
ORANGE 02		Adding a warm brown undertone creates a rich, earthy effect which is more of a mid-saturation, meaning it feels peaceful, comforting and relaxing.
ORANGE 03		The lightest of the three, Orange 03 shares Orange 02's warm brown undertones but the addition of grey makes it more muted (and therefore a much lower saturation). This would benefit subtler schemes, the warmth working well in social spaces to encourage conversation.

@sandradieckmann; ceiling in Yellow 02, walls in White 03, door in Orange 01

Colour insight: orange

Vincent van Gogh – one of the world's greatest painters – extensively featured orange in his work, from his sunflower series to his depictions of wheat fields, as well as within his own self-portraits, to represent his orange hair.

Interestingly, he created many of his most orange-toned, visually lighter and brighter pieces during the times he was said to be at his happiest, while those painted during his well-documented depressive periods tend to be more muted and cooler toned. Perhaps – whether consciously or not – his use of orange was also conveying his headspace at the time of painting.

Deep dive: yellow

COLOUR TYPE

Primary colour; psychological primary

KEY ATTRIBUTES

Uplifting, creative, happy, optimistic
and positive. Yellow can directly affect
our emotions and impact our nervous
system, so choose it and use it with care.

IDEAL FOR

Hallways or bathrooms. For places you only
spend a limited time in while coming and
going, an abundant smothering of yellow
is instantly welcoming and gives a short,
sharp hit of the feel-goods. For a similar
effect, use it on a ceiling for an on-demand
mood boost (just look up).

This warm primary, and its tints, tones and shades,
really brings the summer vibes, whatever the
weather. Depending on the variations and quantities
you choose, it can feel calm and soothing or
invigorating. Simply being in yellow's company
can make us feel confident, positive and content.

Yellow is also great at reflecting light around a room:
as the brightest hue in the visible spectrum, our
eyes read it as the most noticeable of all colours.
The qualities it emanates – cosy, warm, joyful and
energetic – are everything we want our homes to
have. Both the Lick community and many of my
clients are really embracing yellow kitchens right
now, which sort of proves this point; often the social
hub of the home, it makes sense to decorate them in
a colour that shares this characteristic.

It's worth treating yellow with a little caution,
however: you can't simply 'turn it off' if it feels too
intense in certain spaces. Use a highly saturated
tone in the wrong setting, and you might not always
appreciate its almost shouty level of joy (it could
even tip into anxiety-inducing territory). Mitigate
this by opting for a lower intensity instead, such
as a calming, creamier equivalent.

Three personalities of yellow

Lick's pick	Mood	How it works
		This bright, energetic yellow is like daubing a splash of warm sunlight directly onto your walls. Its white and gold undertones contribute to its radiancy, and can instil feelings of optimism. As it's SO highly saturated, I usually suggest using this as an accent so its energy doesn't become too full-on.
		With its warm brown and grey undertones, Yellow 07 is far less saturated, meaning it sits at the soothing end of the scale. This gives it a more earthy, mellow feel, which is easier to live with on a larger scale.
		The addition of red undertones creates a richer mid-saturation yellow, which mixes red's happy vibes with yellow's confidence.

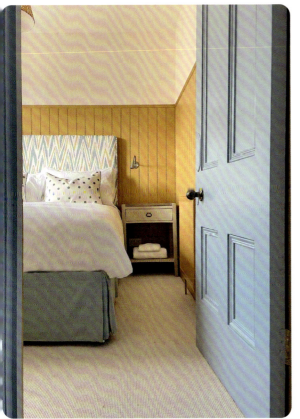

Colour insight: yellow

At Lick, yellow is starting to give pink a run for its money as a new neutral. We're seeing more and more of our community members choose creamier tones like pale yellow, or white with a heavy yellow pigment, which they are layering on with our brighter yellows to really make it pop.

I think there are many reasons for this shift, but it's ultimately down to yellow's warm and welcoming feel, and a desire to use it as an antidote to what have been a difficult few years for so many of us.

Deep dive: green

COLOUR TYPE

Secondary; psychological primary

KEY ATTRIBUTES

Balancing, refreshing, growth, restful and thought-provoking. Considered nature's neutral, surrounding yourself in it can feel safe and restorative.

IDEAL FOR

Any room, basically! You can't really go wrong with green, it's just about finding the perfect shade for you and the room you're decorating.

Falling slap bang in the middle of the colour spectrum, green is quite literally easy on the eye, as its position means it takes little to no adjustment for us to process it (our eyes can see more shades of green than any other colour, from zesty mints to earthy olives). As such, it's considered restful and soothing (and consistently ranks as the world's second-favourite colour in various surveys – usually pipped to the post by its neighbour, blue). Joining red, yellow and blue as one of the four psychological colour primaries, it has an ability to balance red's physicality, blue's intellect and yellow's emotions.

You can't really talk about the psychology of green without mentioning biophilia, which was brought to international attention over 40 years ago by biologist Dr Edward Wilson. His research confirmed there's an inherent human desire (and need) to engage with and feel connected to nature on a deep, primal level, and studies have shown that simply looking at images of nature can bring us a level of biophilic benefit. So while painting your walls a lush forest green won't soothe the soul quite as much as an actual walk through the woods, psychologically it's a nod in the right direction.

Three personalities of green

Lick's pick	Mood	How it works
GREEN 08		The yellow undertone in this fresh green is what's powering its vibrancy and giving it a jolt of energy, while the addition of a cool blue undertone creates a fresh, minty look. This high-saturation combination can help you feel a little more awake (thanks to the yellow), while the blue undertone can enhance free thinking.
GREEN 19		This mix of brown and yellow undertones creates a dark yet warm mid-saturation tone, which balances brown's restorative properties with yellow's stimulation, creating a colour that will help you feel rejuvenated.
GREEN 01		This soft, low-saturation sage green contains warm yellow undertones, yet compared to Green 08 its appearance is gentler due to the absence of blue. Rooms incorporating this tone will therefore feel more restful and soothing (even with that dash of energising yellow), and have a strong biophilic association.

Deep dive: blue

COLOUR TYPE

Primary colour; psychological primary

KEY ATTRIBUTES

Calming, tranquil, inviting, honest and safe. Blue's stress-busting abilities inspire feelings of serenity and contentment.

IDEAL FOR

I always recommend using a light, soothing tone here to clients who struggle with sleep (it's the best option as it relaxes the body and helps the brain prepare to switch off). Darker tones are also great in a home office or study area, as they are said to encourage productivity and focus.

Generally considered the world's most popular colour, it'd be easy to assume that's simply because it's a pleasant and easy hue to live with – but there's a lot more to it than that. It's thought that we have a more positive (rather than neutral or negative) bias towards blue than any other colour, as we associate it so closely with nature – as such, it provides a sense of the familiar (which in turn can feel comforting).

Blue's psychological primary relates to intellect, meaning our brain tends to find lighter blues mentally soothing, while its darker variants can provide more mental stimulation (hence the term 'blue-sky thinking', which generally refers to open-minded, creative brainstorming).

A key criticism of blue is that it can feel cold and uninviting, though while it's certainly on the cool side of the colour wheel, there are plenty of ways to make it feel warmer and cosier, from your choice of undertones and its saturation, to what else you pair it with. Adding it to living spaces simultaneously feels dramatic and comforting: darker hues like teal and navy add warmth, while lighter shades create a soothing ambiance.

Three personalities of blue

Lick's pick	Mood	How it works
BLUE 01		The low saturation levels in this blue mean its relationship to its blue parent-primary is less obvious than Blue 10, and its grey undertones keep it cool. This creates a colour that's mentally soothing and can help make a space feel brighter and more open.
BLUE 07		Blue 07 almost takes this in the opposite direction, its heavy saturation creating a rich, dark inky shade, reminiscent of the night sky. This provides the clarity of mind that blue always brings, while its intensity makes it more mentally stimulating than paler tones.
BLUE 10		Blue 10 could be considered the most 'pure' of these three – it's the most obviously 'blue' at a glance due to its high saturation. As a mid-powder blue, it feels both crisp and warm due to its respective white and yellow undertones. Its saturation makes it stimulating, meaning it's a good fit for rooms where you wish to feel energised and creative.

Deep dive: pink

COLOUR TYPE

Tint

KEY ATTRIBUTES

Soothing, affectionate, sensitive, caring and nurturing. Coming home to pink can feel like walking into a cosy embrace and being handed a comforting cup of tea.

IDEAL FOR

Spaces you want to feel cocooned in, whether that's a personal space like a bedroom or bathroom, or a social area like a family den. Use it in a hallway and you'll get that warm hug as soon as you step through the door.

Pink is one of those shoulder-dropping colours: if you walk into a room that's decked out in it, you can just feel your shoulders instantly drop and your whole body relax. Colour-curious members of the Lick community often choose pink and green schemes as their gateway into colour, as the two complement each other so well, while lighter pinks are increasingly used as a 'new neutral'.

The personality traits of pink are basically toned-down versions of red, so in turn it evokes physical responses depending on its tone and intensity. But for a colour that's largely tender and loving, it can be surprisingly divisive. A lot of this comes down to social conditioning, but in the last decade, the popularity of 'millennial pink' helped shake off the gender clichés, with earthy tones proving popular across the home.

However, too much pink can tip its nurturing qualities into energy-sapping territory, which can feel draining. Find the right tone for your space and mood goals, and you'll strike the perfect balance.

Three personalities of pink

Lick's pick	Mood	How it works
PINK 01		Heavily diluted with white, Pink 01 also contains a touch of grey, which knocks out some of its sweetness. This creates a cool, low-saturation colour that's still soothing and nurturing but also acts as a super-versatile neutral.
PINK 07		An earthy pink with a dose of both desaturating grey and warm brown undertones creates a mid-saturation colour, which would also work as a darker neutral.
PINK 12		This heavily saturated pink certainly packs a punch, with warm orange and yellow undertones giving it energy and vibrancy. It works well as a visual pick-me-up.

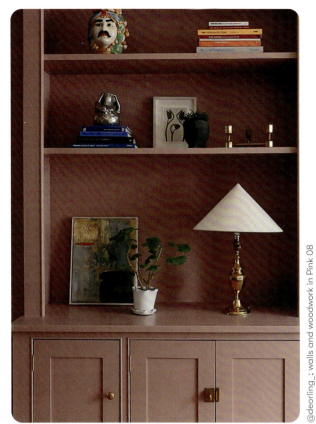

Deep dive: purple

COLOUR TYPE

Secondary

KEY ATTRIBUTES

Contemplative, curious, wise, sophisticated and intriguing. Purple has the power to both stimulate and smooth, and is rarely boring.

IDEAL FOR

Bedrooms – opting for soft purples with a pink undertone can help create a restful haven. I also love using deep, rich purple in a small downstairs cloakroom or WC to add a touch of unexpected drama, especially in a slightly reflective eggshell finish, which helps bounce the light around the space.

Blending two opposing primaries (warm red and cool blue), purple can produce a beautiful array of shades. These variations can incite quite different emotional responses: red-parent purples such as light mauves and dark damsons allude to luxury and power, while on the cooler, blue-parent side we find relaxing lavenders and rich amethysts. Purple can enhance calm and contemplation, while sparking curiosity and creativity (though in the wrong setting it can tip into introspection, or leave us feeling disconnected from reality).

Technically, what we call 'purple' is actually violet, and it's the shortest wavelength our eyes can detect, sitting at the end of the rainbow (i.e. the visible spectrum) – hence its links with the supernatural and spirituality. It's often associated with complex, mystical characters (think *Batman*'s Joker and *The Little Mermaid*'s Ursula). But the late pop legend Prince, who famously embraced the colour wholeheartedly, almost embodied its contradictions: considered a boundary-pushing creative genius who oozed sex appeal, off-stage he was said to be incredibly sensitive, perfectionistic and shy. His preferred shade of purple, which straddles red and blue, nods to these two contrasts.

Three personalities of purple

Lick's pick	Mood	How it works
PURPLE 05		A nuanced-neutral, this light, muted purple has a very low saturation. Warm undertones of pink, grey and white give it an understated, soft and soothing feel.
PURPLE 06		With its warm pink and grey undertones, this pale lilac has a calm, supportive quality that encourages creativity and contemplation.
PURPLE 03		There's no question as to whether this dark velvety purple has a high saturation or not: with blue and yellow undertones, it oozes cosiness and sophistication, and can bring a warming, luxurious feel to rooms.

Colour insight: purple

You might have heard before that the colour purple is related to wealth and royalty, but do you know why? This association arose as the natural pigments required to create purple paints and dyes (before the advent of manufactured synthetic pigment) were extremely labour-intensive – and therefore costly – to produce, making purple the preserve of only the wealthiest in society. The source of purple pigment actually came from a far less glamorous source: the secretions of sea snails, of which thousands were required to create a modest amount.

Deep dive: brown

COLOUR TYPE

Shade

KEY ATTRIBUTES

Reassuring, stable, honest, warm and authentic. Brown brings an old-world charm and understated refinement, and is happy to take the back seat and let other colours shine.

IDEAL FOR

Small living spaces or dens – brown's reassuring warmth can make you feel safe and cosy. Lighter tones also work wonderfully in bedrooms, giving a reassuring vibe without feeling too heavy.

If you tried the Perfect Palette exercise in the last chapter (see page 45), you'll already know that brown is a shade rather than a hue, and it doesn't appear on the basic colour wheel (or in the rainbow). But brown is, in a sense, the original paint colour: the earliest examples of art, found in prehistoric cave paintings, were all made from earth pigments and iron oxides. Perhaps this is why words like 'grounding' feel so synonymous with it.

Like its close cousin orange, brown fell out of favour after the 1970s, but has been enjoying a resurgence in recent years. Google searches for 'brown paint' and 'dark brown paint' increased by 25% and 35% respectively during 2023 and 2024, and the Lick community has been embracing its glow-up from the preserve of rustic and rural schemes into luxurious, timeless looks.

It can sometimes have a bad wrap for being boring, but sometimes we need the safety and comfort this hot-chocolate shade brings to the table. I predict we'll see this shade become even more popular in the coming years, in line with the growing popularity of biophilic design and a general shift away from cooler looks in favour of warm, earthy schemes.

Three personalities of brown

Lick's pick	Mood	How it works
BEIGE 03		This soft, earthy beige balances cool grey and warm yellow undertones to create a relaxing neutral. As a member of the brown family, it has a grounding quality that will bring a comforting, cosy feel to a room, putting you at ease.
BEIGE 02		With a slightly stronger saturation level than its beige neighbour, this colour sits on the warmer side thanks to its mellow yellow and lively red undertones. But as the overall colour is still soft and earthy, it has more of a cocooning, restful feel compared to more saturated browns.
BROWN 02		An earthy dark brown, the intensity of this colour and the inclusion of a red undertone creates a more stimulating feel that is still grounding, cosy and comfortable.

Deep dive: grey

COLOUR TYPE

Neutral

KEY ATTRIBUTES

Dignified, stable, clean, understated and effortless. An endlessly versatile colour, there really is a grey for every person and every mood.

IDEAL FOR

Spaces where you want to create an intimate feel – darker tones especially can create a cocooning, protective ambience. Light greys with warm undertones can feel calming in a bedroom.

It's easy to think of grey as drab, but that does this surprisingly versatile shade a disservice. In its purest form, grey is simply a combination of pure white and pure black, but mixing in other undertones wakes it up: adding lavender or pink undertones to a lighter grey creates a low-saturation, gently soothing tint, while darker greys with a shot of blue or green produce gorgeous rich, moody tones that look super stylish and dramatic.

Grey-on-grey interiors pretty much dominated the last decade decorating-wise, providing an undemanding backdrop to our busy lives. But once the Covid pandemic hit – and many of us spent more time at home than ever – losing so much external stimulation from our lives meant those grey walls suddenly started to feel draining. More vibrant, energising colours and nature-inspired earthy tones became more appealing options to surround ourselves with and support our moods.

Today, grey tends to crop up more in a supporting role rather than a main character, lifting the other colours around it – think a dark flash of contrasting woodwork, or a luxe backdrop for jewel-toned furniture and accessories.

Three personalities of grey

Lick's pick	Mood	How it works
GREY 01		With its cool sky-blue undertones, Grey 01 appears pared-back but has a touch of grit to it. This light grey has a soothing nature and, despite its light tone, can create a cosy retreat vibe.
GREY 14		Although appearing visually cooler than Grey 01, the two share a similar level of saturation, while a drop of warm pink in its undertone takes it out of cold territory and lends it a soft, nurturing air.
GREY 08		Velvet soft, this cool charcoal grey contains blue undertones, yet the depth and intensity of its saturation gives it a somewhat glamorous persona that can make a room feel rich yet relaxing.

Colour insight: grey

When I'm speaking with clients, I notice those who are less confident with colour tend to default to grey, especially for expensive furniture purchases like a sofa. And it totally makes sense; you might be living with that choice for a decade or more, and items like sofas, beds and built-in furniture take up large areas of a room.

But I often find that once I've helped them understand how colour works a little better, their confidence increases, and going for the deep teal or burnt orange sofa that they really love, but would have been too nervous to invest in before, becomes an empowering option.

Deep dive: black

COLOUR TYPE

Neutral

KEY ATTRIBUTES

Glamorous, dramatic, mysterious, grounded and chic. There's no beating around the bush when it comes to black.

IDEAL FOR

Kitchens – pairing black cabinets with off-white walls looks timeless and elegant. Or for an unexpected wow factor, go bold and use it to colour drench a small downstairs cloakroom or WC.

Black's not a shade to shy away from: its deeply dramatic appearance and air of moody mystique tends to demand our attention. A popular maxim in the interiors world is that every room needs a touch of black, whether that's a tiny trim (like a black picture frame or the edging on a cushion) or something a little more substantial, such as a painted bookcase or a statement black ceiling (which looks SO chic, especially under candlelight). This may well stem from the art world, where black is often used to define and draw attention to certain elements, or to add drama and contrast. As such, it can be great at visually anchoring a room.

That's not to say you can't use it on a larger scale, though: it can look sensational when used across all four walls, ceilings and woodwork to colour drench a room, if the tone and the setting is right. Black absorbs all light and reflects nothing back, so – as with grey – I'd usually recommend softening it with an undertone to ensure it doesn't look too heavy (especially when using across larger areas).

A common misconception is that black is a bad choice for small rooms, but with a rich undertone it can transform these areas into a cosy haven. And despite its drama, it can create an incredibly calming, relaxing vibe when styled the right way, with its ability to shut out the rest of the world, inviting you to sit and be engulfed by its elegance.

Two personalities of black

Lick's pick	Mood	How it works
		We've recently reduced our range of blacks to just two at Lick as we think these streamlined options offer everything you could need from a black. The cooler choice, Black 01, pairs cool graphite with inky blue undertones, which brings a little of that black drama. These tones can create a look that fosters feelings of confidence and self-assurance.
		You should be able to spot the subtle yet important temperature difference here compared to Black 01. The second of our two blacks has, in contrast, a warm temperature due to its red undertones, which can create a softer finish and bring a decadent feel.

@the_house_on_the_grapevine; walls in White 04 and Black 01

Colour insight: black

Black has become a popular interiors choice in the last decade or so, but its use in the home dates back to prehistoric times, when the charcoal produced from fire was used to draw or create decorative markings on cave walls.

It was also used to great effect during the Renaissance period from the 14th to 17th centuries, where esteemed Italian artists favoured a painting style called chiaroscuro, which played with dramatic extremes of light to create depth and evoke intense emotions.

Deep dive: white

COLOUR TYPE

Neutral

KEY ATTRIBUTES

Pure, minimal, clean, simple and crisp. A lick of white paint can often feel like a fresh start (painting over grubby, faded white walls with a crisp new white is INCREDIBLY satisfying), while warmer whites bring a welcoming feel.

IDEAL FOR

Every home! There's a perfect white for everyone (and any setting), whether you're after a warm, calming tone or a fresh Scandi feel (it's all about finding the right undertone and balancing it with the natural light entering the space).

White is often the default colour when decorating, which isn't necessarily a bad thing; in some instances, a bright white can look absolutely beautiful in the home. And if you're not colour confident, turning to white can understandably feel like a safer choice, compared to painting your walls in dark or vibrant tones. It's also an obvious option for anyone wanting their home to feel light and airy, as it's so good at reflecting light around a space (and you literally can't get lighter than a pure white).

But this is where it gets interesting: when it comes to the pure brilliant white paint we decorate with, paint manufacturers add brightening pigments to artificially create this purity, resulting in a white that's brighter and slightly cooler than a 'true' pure white colour we'd find naturally. This means white can, in some settings, appear cold, clinical and artificial.

That's why it's crucial to opt for a white that contains one or more undertones, to add depth and softness. When the right white is layered with other colours, materials and patterns it can really come into its own and create a far more homely feel.

Three personalities of white

Lick's pick	Mood	How it works
WHITE 01		With the lightest touch of grey in its undertones, White 01 is sophisticated and cool. Its light-reflecting properties can help bring clarity to both your mind and space.
WHITE 06		A noticeably warmer tone with just a touch more saturation, this white is warmed up with a delicate drop of pink in its undertones, giving it a cosier feel.
WHITE 05		This stone white contains warm yellow undertones, giving it a creamy, comforting tone that feels welcoming and relaxing.

@newformdesign.uk; walls in White 05, units in Green 02

@renovationhq walls in White 05

2

Analyse:
what inspires you?

By now you'll have a far better understanding of how to choose colours to create both the look and feeling you want. But what I'd love you to do next is try out the exercises here with fresh eyes, and turn the tables on yourself: how does what you've learnt so far fit in with what you already knew about your colour preferences? Has it reaffirmed some of your previous colour choices, or are you now looking at everything in a different light?

This quest to help you uncover your own perfect palette is going to go beyond interiors: I'll be asking you to analyse the aesthetics of a few key areas in your life, to see if they challenge your preconceptions or help you spot instances where you've been following trends rather than trusting your instincts.

So, keep an open mind and answer these questions honestly. We're not looking for conclusions at this stage, we're simply fact-finding to build up a bigger picture (and you'll be able to channel these insights into the interiors decisions we'll come to later on).

You can write out your answers in a notebook (or digital app of your choice), or scan the QR code on this page to get a printable version of the questions. Ready?!

Assess your wardrobe

+ Open your wardrobe doors and take a glance. What are the main colours and patterns in there? Write them down, making a rough note of what they are and what percentage of your wardrobe they take up.

+ Next, look at your accessories (whether that's shoes, jewellery, bags or hats). Do these tell a different story? How do they relate to your wardrobe (for example, do you tend to wear lots of black but dress it up with colourful statement necklaces, or do you often go fully tonal, down to your socks and scarf?)

+ Which pieces make you feel your best? Why is that? Is it their colour, fit or material?

+ Which pieces tend to be your default if you're feeling down? Again, ask yourself why – and what the differences (or similarities) are between this answer and the one above?

Look to nature

+ If temperature wasn't a factor, what would your favourite beach view look like? Would it be vibrant blue skies and bright golden sands, or a moody and windswept day where everything is desaturated? Maybe you're viewing the beach at dusk, with that magical twilight glow in the air?

+ Think about somewhere you go regularly, and how this looks across the seasons. Ask yourself which season feels the most 'you'. Is it the pastels of spring? The vibrant tones and abundant colours of summer? Those warm, rich, earthy hues found in autumn? Or the stark, moody contrasts most prevalent in winter?

Mentally revisit your favourite places

+ Think about your favourite coffee shop or restaurant, or a really special place you've visited. Why was it special? What feelings did it evoke? Was it cosy and welcoming? Light and airy? Did it feel fancy or homely?

+ Where's the most beautiful place you've visited? Why have you chosen this place? Think about both the aesthetics and how it made you feel.

Go on a colour hunt

Whether you make a special trip or simply carve out time to try this when you're next out and about, I'd love you to go for a 'colour hunt' to round all of this off. It could be an outing to a favourite destination or simply a walk around the block (in fact, the latter can be a really helpful challenge – it's sometimes harder to spot something beautiful or unique in the familiar and everyday).

Make notes as you go, or, even better, take photos and add a comment against each photo file to reference later. Try to spot:

+ A colour that catches your eye. Why has it drawn your attention? Do you like or dislike it?

+ A colour you LOVE. What kind of colour is it? Can you spot its main characteristics? Is it warm or cool? High or low saturation? What might its undertones be?

+ A colour you dislike (ask yourself the same questions as for the colour you love).

+ An interesting colour combination: say, the different tones in the cobbled stone paving you're walking on, or the colour of the trees against the sky just as the sun is popping out after a rain shower. How do you feel about this combination?

Mary's fashion-influenced townhouse

Mary is the epitome of cool. She is a fashion trendsetter and influences culture with her music. As a model and DJ, she has lots of first-hand experience putting together different colours, patterns and styles when it comes to clothes, but was struggling to work out how to translate this into her home.

While she had a clear vision of the overall vibe and feel she wanted to create – and had already made a strong start on the overall design of the space – as a first-time home renovator, she lacked decorating confidence and couldn't quite see how to bring together all the bright colours she loves without it feeling chaotic. She had keenly observed how colours can affect your mood, and loves how dressing in vibrant colours makes her feel, so it was key that we approached her home colour choices with this ethos in mind.

What you'll see throughout her finished home is that although we chose a lot of strong colours, tonally they all sit together perfectly, which always creates harmony however bright you go. Where we've used neutrals, these all sit sympathetically with the bolder colours, for a look that's considered and strong but not overwhelming.

We made a conscious decision to create a relatively light and airy feel downstairs, using White 02 across both the walls, ceiling and skirting boards (its balanced grey undertones really complement the exposed brick and oak flooring), then treated her kitchen units – which sit in the middle of the space – almost like a jewellery box, with punchy, contrasting tones of royal blue and putty pink.

Mary really liked the idea of using red for her main guest bedroom. While a strong red would likely feel

WHO LIVES HERE?

Mary Charteris, a model and DJ, alongside husband Robbie, and daughter Wilde.

INSTAGRAM

@marycharteris

THE PROPERTY

A Victorian townhouse spread over four floors. The ground floor has been extended at the back to create a large, light-filled kitchen/dining/family space, allowing the original living room to function as an intimate snug. On the second floor is the primary guest room and main bathroom. The third floor is taken over by the couple's bedroom suite (incorporating their bedroom, dressing area and en suite). The top floor houses Wilde's bedroom and a second guest bedroom.

PREFERRED COLOURS AND STYLES

Vibrant jewel tones with a bit of rock chick. Mary's palette is bold and energising, but laid-back when it needs to be.

too overwhelming in a sleeping space, we settled on Red 03, which is actually quite grounding due to its warm brown and pink undertones. This looked stunning colour-drenched across her built-in wardrobes and over the ceiling, and created a real cocooning effect. Bringing in tiny touches of black – in the cupboard handles, light fittings and bedframe – gave it that slight edge that she wanted.

In Mary and Robbie's bedroom suite, she really wanted to go to town and, as a more private area than the main living spaces, this made perfect sense. She made some really brave colour choices, and it totally paid off. While the bedroom itself is tranquil and tonal, with walls and skirting both painted in pale Blue 01, a harmonious Teal 01 on the fitted wardrobes, and repeating the White 02 used downstairs on the ceiling, her floorboards have been finished in a bold purple shade. This shakes things up, but it works SO well as purple sits next to blue on the colour wheel, meaning the two share tonal similarities. Keeping this bold colour pop on the floor allows the rest of the room to retain its tranquil feel.

This all hints at what's to come in the dressing room, which leads directly off the sleeping space and is where Mary's inner rock chick really comes out: the tendency with dark, windowless spaces is to paint them white, but here she's played on the darkness by totally colour drenching the space in a heavily saturated green with a high gloss finish, which looks amazing against the leopard-print carpet. This leads through to their bold en-suite bathroom, painted in a vibrant warm blue (Lick's Blue 10 is very similar), with a gently curved vintage mirror adding softness and character to this small space.

Mary's core house palette

KEY PARENT COLOURS

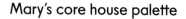

LEADING LICK PAINT PICKS

| WHITE 02 | BLUE 01 | TEAL 01 | GREEN 08 | RED 03 | TEAL 03 |

'I love how the dark blue kitchen units seem to come alive when the morning sun hits them – choosing an eggshell finish really helps with this, as it bounces even more light around. While my house certainly has a lot of colours in it, I don't find it overwhelming at all. Guests love coming here and say it has a real party vibe, yet it also feels relaxing.'

– MARY –

Understanding your home

We've talked a lot so far about how colour works in both practical and psychological terms; now let's start to put all of that into practice. In this chapter, I'll help you get to know your home a little better so you can choose the colours to create a scheme that will suit any of its rooms.

Often when we consider which colours to use in a room, we tend to go straight in with an arbitrary choice – such as deciding to paint it grey, or believing we can't paint it green as that 'won't work'. In fact, choosing the best colours for the space you want to decorate comes down to a number of factors (not to mention the psychology-based personalities of each paint). You'll often stumble across articles online which give sweeping statements and fixed, blanket rules, like you can't use blue in a small room, or red is bad for bedrooms. However, you can use any colour in any room – it's just about understanding the factors that will alter its look.

First we'll look at the light coming into your home – remember that how we see colour is through light, so light is the most important consideration when it comes to choosing colours for your home. We'll then look at other factors which affect this, such as what artificial light does and how to get this right, and how the quality of light typically received depending on where you are in the world can affect which colours work best.

By bearing in mind the aspects you can and can't change, you'll be able to work around or mitigate flaws and turn them into features: for example, turning a gloomy north-facing room into a cosy jewel-toned retreat.

We'll also explore some common housing types, review their good points and flaws, assess the fixed elements you might not be able to change and look at how you can work with, rather than against, them. Finally, we'll get a little more practical and look at examples of each room in a typical home, exploring different ways to choose colour and decorate them.

So, if you do want to paint your small, gloomy living room dark blue, contrary to popular opinion you absolutely can – but you need to find the right colour to ensure it feels warm and inviting.

You'll be able to apply what you've learned and make the best choices with your own home's DNA as well as your own personal preferences in mind. With the help of some useful exercises, I'll help you to pull all of this together and create your perfect palette.

Light and its effect on colour

When making colour choices across all elements in a room, including flooring and furnishings as well as paint, this generally comes down to fixed factors (things you can't change), lifestyle factors (things you have a degree of control over) and choosing pigment-rich paints (which you definitely have a say in!).

Here's how they all work together:

Fixed factors: does your room faces north, south, east or west? How much light comes into the space? For example, is the sun obscured by a nearby tree or neighbouring wall? Is the light affected by how far it is from ground level (whether it's in a basement flat or a high-rise block)?

Lifestyle factors: what times of day do you use this space? Is it where you wake up in the morning, sit while you eat lunch, or wind down in the evening? Does it support your needs at these times, such as energising you for the day ahead, or relaxing you before bedtime? Are there other times you'd like to use it, but it just doesn't seem as appealing due to feeling dull and gloomy or too bright?

I'll walk you through some of this in more detail when we get to this chapter's Perfect Palette exercise on pages 122–123, but starting to think about all of this now might unearth some useful insights that could even change how you use the space entirely.

For example, if you find your kids are ignoring their playroom in favour of the main living area as it's lighter and more spacious, could you consider switching these around and turn their playroom into your cosy TV den instead? Do you tend to eat breakfast sitting on the sofa because your kitchen chairs aren't actually comfy and are squashed in an awkward corner, when a better seating solution could make this a more practical and appealing option?

Pigments, light and the personality of paint

There's a lot more to paint than just the colour that we see and how it interacts with the light around it: how it is manufactured also plays a large part in how we perceive it. Commercially mixed paints are created in a similar way to the colour mixing exercises we worked on in chapter one – except rather than adding white, black or grey to an existing colour, the process starts with a white base, which different quantities of coloured particles (known as pigments) are added to, which includes grey and black, along with a range of other hues.

These pigments not only create the paint's final colour, they're also what gives it its depth, vibrancy and personality, allowing it to respond and react to the light it receives, altering its appearance and attitude as the day progresses. Cheaper paints tend to use fewer pigments in limited quantities, which can result in colours that look dull, flat and lifeless; conversely, premium paints will use more varied pigments in greater quantities, creating deliciously nuanced shades which have a luminous feel (I always describe this as if the sun were dancing across your room throughout the day).

A global note

This book describes light in relation to the northern hemisphere, so if you're reading this in the southern hemisphere, firstly – hi! And secondly, be aware that the seasons and light orientation are opposite. For example, the characteristics of a north-facing room in the northern hemisphere will be the opposite for you, meaning your north-facing rooms will share the same properties as my south-facing rooms, and vice versa.

Teal 01 is one of those colours that really shows the magic of pigment-rich paint. These two photos of Lucinda, from This Hove Home's north-facing bedroom and Victoria Covell's east-facing kitchen demonstrate beautifully why I love it so much: its green tones really pop in Victoria's kitchen when the bright morning sun hits it, while in the indirect daylight of Lucinda's bedroom the blue tones become more prominent because of how it reacts with a cooler, greyer light coming in (which is also really relaxing for sleep). I don't think you could ever get bored of a colour that provides so much variation throughout the day.

TEAL 01

Making the most of sunlight

There's a bit of a misconception about 'good' and 'bad' room orientations, and estate agents often boast about south-facing rooms but fail to give north-facing ones the same level of enthusiasm. Actually, no orientation is 'bad'; the trick is to lean into every room's inherent characteristics rather than fight against them, in order to find the perfect balance between what suits the space and what meets your needs.

For a north-facing room – which will naturally fall on the duller side – help it come to life with a rich mid-toned colour that can create a cosy, soulful feel, rather than trying to trick it into looking bright by painting it white (which will likely just look bland and dreary). If you've got a sun-filled, south-facing room, using lighter tones and brighter colours can open up the space and allow its gorgeousness to sing.

If your room is dual aspect (so has light coming from different directions), or sits on the cusp of two different compass points, observe how the light behaves throughout the day as well as considering how and when you use the space, and adapt this advice accordingly. If in doubt, stick to green and pink tones, which can be the best options for balancing different types of light. Another useful rule of thumb is to remember that balanced colours (those containing both cool and warm undertones, such as yellow and grey) will work in pretty much any orientation, while colours skewed towards one side or the other might work best in more specific circumstances.

North-facing rooms

Lighting type: indirect and even across the day (you won't get any direct sunlight coming through the windows, and therefore shadows will be minimal, too).

West-facing rooms

Lighting type: cooler and more subdued during the morning, becoming lighter and more intense across the afternoon. Leading up to sunset, you'll be treated to glorious 'golden hour' sunlight, so-called because of the reduced-intensity rich red and gold wavelengths the sun emits as it lowers in the sky.

East-facing rooms

Lighting type: soft, direct bright sunlight in the morning, which becomes indirect across the afternoon and evening. Bedrooms and breakfast nooks blessed with this orientation will get a welcome hit of energising sunshine first thing, helping to kick-start your day.

South-facing rooms

Lighting type: bright, direct light for most of the day. On sunny days the room can be flooded with light, which makes contrasts and shadows more noticeable.

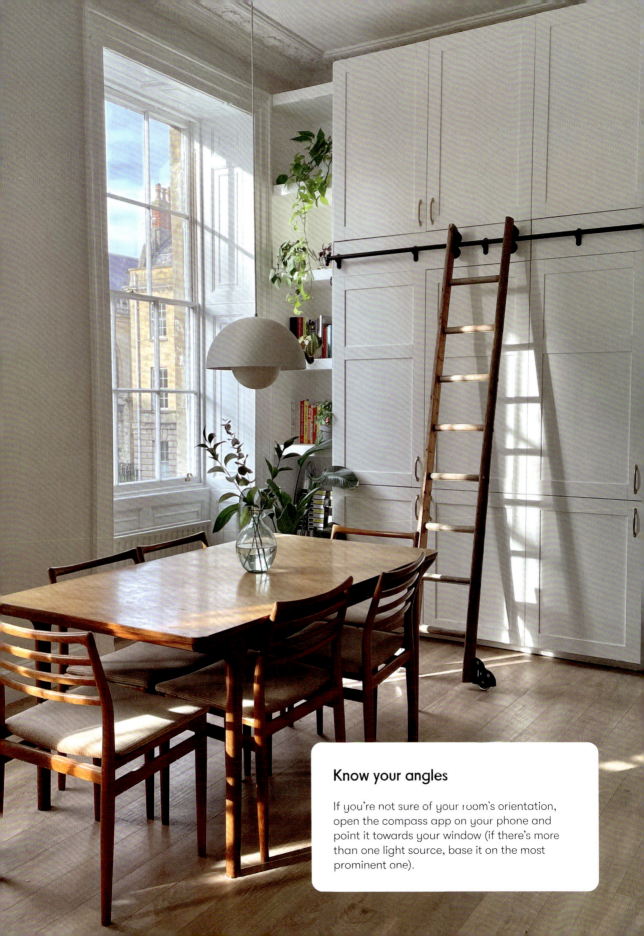

Know your angles

If you're not sure of your room's orientation, open the compass app on your phone and point it towards your window (if there's more than one light source, base it on the most prominent one).

One colour, four orientations

North-facing

How to decorate: balance out the naturally grey tones of this light by using colours with warm undertones. You might be able to go brighter than you think, as colours can appear toned down. North-facing rooms offer consistency over drama, which can feel reassuring, and their steady natural light can take both deeper tones and lighter neutrals (many artists and photographers prefer north-facing studios for these reasons).

East-facing

How to decorate: colours will appear brighter in the morning, becoming duller once the sun moves higher in the sky. For rooms you use more in the morning – like a bedroom – choosing colours with warm undertones is key, so they feel vibrant and bright in the morning as you prepare for the day ahead but don't then turn overly cold in the evening.

PINK 02

While many of our paint colours work in more than one room orientation, Pink 02 really is a stalwart, and manages to just look amazing in any space. Its versatility comes from its neutrality: as a light-weight colour, its warm yellow and grey undertones give it a peachy look, which feels grounding as either a backdrop or an accent. This allows it to maximise whatever natural light happens to hit it, creating a feel that's simultaneously fresh and soothing.

@buildbysets

South-facing

How to decorate: bright colours will look even more luminous and also appear a little lighter than they really are, so as a general rule, choosing cooler-toned lights and brights will help balance this out and make the most of its sunny properties.

West-facing

How to decorate: some people advise using only cool tones in a west-facing room to balance out this golden-hour glow, but I LOVE going the opposite way and embracing this by using warm, rich, earthy tones in here because when that late light hits – just wow! It can be SO beautiful, it feels unreal (go west, go warm is my motto).

Illuminate your evenings

We tend to focus on how daylight affects our homes, leaving artificial light to play second fiddle. But while lighting serves a practical purpose (illuminating our rooms when it would otherwise be too dark to see), it also plays a crucial role in supporting our moods and emotions. Just as certain colours can stimulate or soothe us, so can lighting.

Light also affects our circadian rhythm (aka our body clock), which picks up cues from the light around us, letting our brains know when it's time to get up and go back to bed. This rhythm doesn't pay much attention to whether that light is coming from the sun, a lightbulb or your phone screen: if you expose yourself to get-up-and-go lighting when it's wind-down-for-bed time, your sleep can be adversely affected. Harsh, strong lighting can leave us feeling on edge, especially for those who are more environmentally sensitive (think of the different lighting approaches between a brightly lit fast food restaurant – which relies on a quick turnover of people – compared to a bistro with its flickering candles and cosy pockets of light, where you're encouraged to linger with a bottle of wine).

Insight

When you're working out the best colours for your room while considering light, think about the time of day you're using the space the most: is it a room you only really use in the evening, and therefore you'll be mainly seeing it under artificial light? Or a space you'll mainly be in during the day, like a home office? If it's one or the other, prioritise your colour choices with this in mind. We'll talk about sampling paint swatches in chapter five, but this is why it's super important to look at colours in the light you'll actually be using them in.

Setting the scene

Just as the sun's light shifts from stronger blue wavelengths during the day to warmer red and orange wavelengths as it sets, you want to try and mimic this effect in your home. You can achieve this in several ways.

I always encourage my clients to use warm, layered lighting in their homes, which creates a lovely glow and gives far more choice and flexibility than relying on a single overhead light (which just instantly kills the mood); you want those little pockets and pools of light for intrigue. Aim for a mix of floor and table lamps, and wall-mounted uplighters, then bring in extra added twinkle from flickering candles.

Lighting technology has improved loads in recent years, making it much easier (and cheaper) to create clever lighting set-ups which don't need electrical rewiring (great for renters and those not wanting the additional hassle). Plug-in flex lights, with an industrial-look lighting cord and a retro-style bare bulb at the end, are lightweight and easy to suspend from wall hooks. Portable lamps make it much easier to add extra lighting to spots where lighting cords would get in the way.

It's also important to look at the colour of your bulbs, too. You might be thinking, they're just white, right? Well, yes, but most 'white' bulbs are either warm or cool toned, with cool white bulbs mimicking that brighter blue daytime light, while warmer, red-toned bulbs are less mentally stimulating. If in doubt, ask yourself: is the light from this bulb similar to the flame on a candle or a gas stove? If it's more like a candle, it's warm.

I always recommend a warm white unless something brighter is needed for specific tasks. If you want a little more flexibility throughout the day, take a look at smart bulbs, which you can adjust in both tone and intensity as needed, through a phone app.

Luke and Fran's bedroom is a great example of three-level lighting, as they have included both wired-in wall lights, a table lamp and a ceiling light. The ceiling light provides general ambient light during a gloomy day, while the table lamps can be used to give a little golden glow as the sun sets. Wall lights are a great option for bedrooms with limited bedside-table space, too.

Colours in your country

Where you are in the world will undoubtedly affect how you decorate your home, from cultural and heritage influences to the housing stock typical of your region. But have you considered how the kind of sunlight in your geographical area influences how you choose and use colours, too?

Put simply, how near or far you are from the equator will impact the quality of daylight you typically receive, which can have a big impact on what colours work best in your locale. Here's how this works in three key regions:

Tropical regions (those closest to the equator):

WHITE 01   GREEN 08   GREEN 07   BLUE 19   ORANGE 01

+ **Natural light:** while tropical countries are hot, and we think of their light as being very warm and yellow, the sun's vibrancy here contains strong blue and white tones, meaning it actually has a cool quality to it.

+ **Colours to use:** this intense light means colours need to be equally bold, bright and highly saturated, as paler or more muted tones will simply look washed out. Pure white works best in this climate (compared to warmer white tints), as it balances the warmth of the sun and can feel physically cooler.

+ **Five key tropical colours:** containing no black pigment, these cheerful tones are energising and can hold their own against strong sunlight.

Temperate regions (countries which are cooler than the tropics, but warmer than the poles):

WHITE 06   TAUPE 03   PINK 08   GREEN 18   GREEN 05

+ **Natural light:** these regions will have more distinct seasons, meaning wildly fluctuating heat and light levels across the year. This can require careful planning to find colours that will work on the dullest midwinter day as well as during the height of a summer heatwave.

+ **Colours to use:** the super-saturated tones more typical of hot climates can look overpowering here, so colours that are a little muddier and knocked-back will work better for a richer and moodier look. If you want to take it light and bright, try a more sun-bleached palette – a little less saturated, this is inspired by the colours on tropical building façades which have been naturally faded by the harsh sun.

+ **Five key temperate colours:** while appearing very different to their tropical counterparts, the main difference between this palette and the previous one is the addition of black pigment, making the colours less saturated and more toned down, giving a more heritage feel.

High Latitude regions (colder countries closer to the north and south poles):

| WHITE 03 | TEAL 01 | BEIGE 02 | BEIGE 10 | BLACK 02 |

+ **Natural light:** the sun sits much lower in the sky in these regions (even during the height of summer), meaning its intensity is low, too. This position means more of its shorter red and orange wavelengths are visible, and the light looks softer and warmer compared to the temperate and tropical regions.

+ **Colours to use:** think typical (and super popular) Scandi-style colour schemes, which use lots of white tints to make the most of the daylight they do receive, but – crucially – mix these with warm, natural materials such as wood alongside tactile soft furnishings like linen and jute to keep it feeling cosy. Black is often used as an accent to give ambiance, in both decorative details and within the paint's pigment to create depth of colour.

+ **Five key cold-country colours:** with its limited range of hues, these five nature-inspired colours all share warm undertones, making them perfect for cooler regions.

Insight

When we launched Lick in the UK, we had an initial palette of 50 colours that bore the British climate in mind. Then as we became international, we doubled this number to create a more globally inclusive palette. My goal as a colour curator is to make sure I can offer the right colours to anyone, wherever they are in the world.

I spent time working with designers in several territories to help me understand how the light works around the globe. While some of our colours tend to work better in certain regions, broadly speaking they can all work anywhere – it's just about finding the right tone and saturation for your space.

Common property-related dilemmas

Every country has its own typical housing stock, whether that's related to the era it was built in or the style of property, but there are often shared similarities (and common problems) to be found between many of them. And having talked to over 5,000 people during my consultations, I understand your pain points pretty well!

In this section, we'll look closely at decorating approaches for different types of rooms. But before we dive in, I want to share a few tips and ideas on some of the decorating and style dilemmas I'm asked about most frequently.

How can I zone an open-plan apartment?

Whether it's a cool industrial warehouse conversion or a simple studio, lateral apartments often feel spacious due to their larger visible footprint. But the lack of walls can prove challenging, and lead to lining the edges of the space with furniture, making it look like a giant waiting room.

Crittall-style glazed partitions – or semi-sheer drapes – can be a clever way to break up the space while still allowing light to shine through. Choose furniture strategically, opting for a modular high-backed sofa, or church pew-style benches at a dining table, to visually contain and define these areas. Then, use colour to support this – large floor rugs can demarcate certain areas, while paint can provide the same function on walls and ceiling, helping visually define one area from another.

@tash_lickcolour; room colour drenched in White 03

@mcclark_bespoke_kitchens; walls and woodwork in Teal 01

Image courtesy of @oak_furniture_land

My house has a dark middle room, what can I do with it?

It's quite common in houses that are three-rooms deep for the middle room to lack natural light (and potentially be a bit gloomy), even if they're part of an open-plan layout. This can make them feel uninviting, or turn them into a thoroughfare between the front and back rooms (rather than anywhere you'd want to stop and linger).

I alway recommend working with nature rather than against it – so if that's the case, take this as an opportunity to lean into it and create a bit of a moment, painting the space in mid-weight or darker colours that have a warm undertone. This will help absorb those grey shadows so its low light levels are less obvious, creating a cosy, welcoming feel. Our eyes travel through pattern, so add interest with bookshelves, art or wallpaper to divert attention from the low light levels. Giving the space a clear purpose (such as adding in a comfy armchair to turn it into a reading nook) will help it feel less like a thoroughfare and more of a destination in its own right.

I love the American-style modern farmhouse aesthetic – how can I recreate this look in my own home?

The Lick community are LOVING this style right now, and it's so timeless and elegant that it's not likely to fall out of favour anytime soon. It blends rustic country charm with a clean, modern aesthetic for a look that's full of character.

I'm a big fan of the American interior design firm Studio McGee (who feature in Netflix's *Dream Home Makeover*). They champion this approach with their trademark warm yet neutral palettes and strong use of texture and subtle country-influenced patterns, like ticking stripe and seersucker. Adding darker touches – say, a deep teal in a seating nook, or painting kitchen units a warm charcoal – brings a sophisticated vibe without it feeling stuffy or formal.

When used in a more traditional rustic property, this approach adds a luxe twist, but in more modern homes it can add character without looking themed.

Kitchens

Room round-ups usually start with the hallway, as that marks the home's beginning. But I prefer to start in the heart of the home: the kitchen. Many of the activities taking place here are naturally loving and nurturing, from perking ourselves up with a morning coffee to cooking something special for loved ones. It's where we make memories, celebrate, and comfort one another.

If your kitchen also incorporates seating, it'll likely host activities from homework to hot-desking around the table, or leisurely weekend breakfasts on a bar stool with the papers. Even tiny kitchens seem to have a social pull that we naturally gravitate towards, whether there are two or twenty of us.

So how do we decorate this space to reflect its nurturing personality? To ensure its practical requirements don't leave it looking clinical and sterile – I suggest approaching it as a continuation of the rest of your home: bring in softer furnishings like upholstered banquette seating, or just a little fabric cocktail chair tucked in a corner, alongside decorative accents such as an art print to break up an expanse of wall, or a lamp on the end of a worktop for a layered lighting effect. Open shelves are practical and can enhance this homely feel, especially when mixing in the odd ornament with your crockery and cookware.

I've advised on thousands of kitchen colour schemes and, in my experience, these rooms work best with light or mid-toned colours on walls, ceilings and woodwork. It's calmer for your eyes and gives the opportunity to bring bolder or darker colour into other areas, such as your kitchen units or those seating and art accents.

Try this:

+ Contrast the colours of base cabinets and wall units for extra interest: take a tonal approach, such as pairing teal with duck egg blue, or opt for a bolder contrast by bringing in punchy pink with grounding sage green. Use the lighter of your colours on the wall units, otherwise it might feel top-heavy.

+ For a small or skinny kitchen, keeping units in light or mid-tones, and close to the wall colour rather than too contrasting, can help avoid the room feeling claustrophobic.

+ If your windows or doors lead directly outside, this is a perfect opportunity to bring the garden into your kitchen by painting the window or door frames green to soften the boundary between the two spaces and create a restful feel.

Crack the colour code

On the next few pages, you'll see arrows against each image to indicate the orientation of the room, so you can get a really good grasp of how this affects the colours you choose.

TIP

Lick paint is designed to go on all surfaces, so if you've inherited kitchen units that are not to your taste, paint them! I'll explain how on page 218.

@belgravehome; walls in White 03

Dark-on-dark kitchens can look stunning in a north-facing space, but contrasting softened blacks with peach-pink walls gives a wonderful warm spin on more classic black-on-white monochrome schemes.

The warmth of this walnut with Red 03 looks so lively when the morning sun hits it – it's like having an extra shot in your coffee!

@_beth_davis; walls in White 06. kitchen units in Green 06

This sun-flooded space benefits from a gentle Blue 04 tone on its units, while the use of warm White 03 on the walls and ceiling helps balance out that potentially harsh southern light.

A dark bottle green provides a punchy contrast to whisper-soft white walls. The delicate pink undertone here helps it sit tonally with the dark wood, too.

Living rooms

Our kitchens might be the hardest working room in the home, but often the living room comes a close second. Unless you're lucky enough to have more than one reception area, you'll need yours to perform multiple jobs throughout the day, from relaxing or pursuing hobbies to working and socialising. Yours might also double as a kids' playroom (mine does, meaning some days my husband and I rarely sit anywhere else).

Understanding when (and how) you use this space is crucial: is it mainly during the day, or only really at night? Or, like me, is it both, but its function switches from a daytime family play space into an adults-only sanctuary in the evening? This will determine what colours you use here (which also links back to lighting). If it's a predominantly daytime space, veering towards light and bright hues might be best. But if you're only really in there after nightfall, something a bit darker and more atmospheric that really pops under artificial light could create the vibe you're after.

Given this room's importance, try to allocate a decent budget to it when renovating. I always say that you can scrimp a little in hallways and bathrooms, but your living room, kitchen and bedroom are the rooms that deserve the most attention. A beautiful cushy sofa and statement piece of art will not only elevate the room, but also bring in both comfort and joy.

You might want your living room to feel calm, but that doesn't necessarily mean using pastels or neutrals. Calm can also come from colour drenching a room (even using bolder colours) as it removes the contrasts between ceilings and walls, giving the eye less to draw its attention. You're not sleeping here, and when you're socialising or entertaining it can create a conversation piece.

Try this:

+ Gallery walls are great in a living room: consider using a bold or darker colour on the wall behind pictures to make them into even more of a feature.

+ If you want to add a bit of colour without overwhelming the space, keep your walls neutral but add a wow-factor to your ceiling with an unexpected contrasting colour (this looks SO cool). Tie its colour in with other accents in your room, such as your sofa cushions or rug, so it doesn't look random.

@designinglilyspad; room colour drenched in Pink 01 Photo: @amiecharlot

A deep velvety teal ramps up the drama and brings warmth to this north-facing space, aided by this punchy coral sofa. These stimulating tones can help spark conversation.

Offering a softer sort of social, using this understated delicate pink across walls, ceilings and woodwork helps soften the shadows in its sloped ceilings, creating a gently cocooning feel.

@lucyalicehome; walls and woodwork in Blue 04

Drawing attention to engaging focal points, such as a pretty fireplace or statement bookshelves, adds an interesting dimension.

This calming mid-blue has a gentle, approachable quality. Pairing it with pops of red and a playful mirror makes it feel more welcoming to sit in and catch those late afternoon rays.

Hallways and entryways

First impressions count, though rather than decorating to impress others, focus on how you can decorate your entry space or hallway to impress and please YOU every time you come and go.

Whatever your style, we all want to feel that shoulder-dropping sense of relaxation as we get through the door, kick off our shoes and greet our family, fur babies or housemates. Equally, we want to feel confident and uplifted when we're on our way out. This makes hallways the perfect spot to inject your personality and set the tone for the rest of your house. As a passing place – rather than somewhere we spend time lingering – you almost want to go out of your way to make it feel really welcoming.

Entry spaces can vary quite dramatically depending on your property type and where you are in the world, from the narrow, dimly lit hallways typical of smaller terraces in the UK to the spacious, light-filled atriums more common in larger American homes. I regularly turn to pink as my go-to palette when I'm helping clients choose colours for this area: it's like coming home to a warm hug, or having a reassuring voice tell you, 'You've got this' as you head out for the day. It also works wonderfully with its colour-wheel opposite, green, which gives a little nod to the world outside.

Hallways can also be a great spot to experiment with colour, especially if you're looking to step out of neutral territory for the first time. A sunny yellow, which might feel overstimulating in a main living space, could offer that perfect level of uplift here. Hallways can be a great gateway into pattern, too: using bold patterned wallpapers helps the eye travel around the space, and you can then strategically pick colours from this pattern to use elsewhere in your home, creating a more unified feel.

Try this:

+ To lighten up a dark hallway, go for a warm white on your walls (anything cool-toned could look uninviting), then paint woodwork in a similar colour a couple of shades darker: by contrast, this will make your walls look brighter.

+ For homes with narrow hallways that have several rooms leading off it, I'd encourage you to paint the doors and woodwork in the same colour as the walls, rather than defaulting to white - it'll make the overall space look far less busy, in turn creating a calming environment when you come home.

+ If your hallway has a staircase, this offers a wonderful opportunity to bring in a bolder or darker colour, to turn it into a bit of a talking point. It's also worth thinking about the colours you've used elsewhere in your home – and how you might bring in elements of this into this space – to set the tone for the rooms to follow.

@lucyalicehome; room colour drenched in White 09

While it might seem like a scary prospect, Reece's hallway shows the power of embracing dark tones in a north-facing small space to create a rich, dramatic look. The deep grey walls help absorb shadows and make all the rooms leading off it look lighter and brighter.

In stark contrast, Lucy's entrance has a very similar architectural style but a completely different look and feel. With its crisp white walls and woodwork (warmed by its gentle lilac undertone), and a striking yellow stair runner, it makes the most of its brighter south-facing light.

@buildbysets; walls in Pink 02 and Botanical 03 wallpaper

Katie and Byron's east-facing entryway looks gorgeous lit up by the morning sun, with its botanical wallpaper helping it to feel connected to the landscape beyond.

Dining spaces

Separate, formal dining rooms have slowly fallen out of favour in recent decades, as modern living tends to favour flexibility over fixed, single-use spaces. And with cooking now viewed as an activity that brings the family or household together (rather than dividing it), this has helped cement the popularity of combining kitchen and dining areas within the same space to act as a creative and inclusive social hub.

So, the set-up might be different, but the dining space itself is going nowhere. In fact, the popularity of hosting dinner parties at home has grown dramatically in the past few years, as rising living costs have made eating out less affordable (Google searches relating to this topic have been surging in the last few years, especially among the under 40s). Whether you have a dedicated dining room or just a small spot for a table and chairs in a spare corner, it provides a wonderful opportunity to create a little ambiance and atmosphere.

I always suggest painting dining spaces in an eggshell finish rather than matt, where possible, as its higher sheen makes it more reflective under artificial light and flickering candle flames, giving an almost magical feel. If yours is mainly used for hosting or special occasions, play up on that by bringing in those deep, rich, darker tones to enhance this vibe.

But if it's needed for everyday meals or mixed uses, where you might want a more neutral look, you can still nod to this feel by keeping your wall colour subtle and incorporating a bold painted ceiling instead (again, I'd encourage using an eggshell finish, for added impact). Not only does it bring the wow factor, it also visually brings the ceiling height down to create a cosy, intimate mood.

Try this:

+ To physically zone a smaller dining area within a larger space, consider building in some banquette seating (with storage if you can, so it's doubly practical), to make it feel more defined and cosier as well as maximising floorspace. If that's not an option, go for benches rather than dining chairs, which you can keep tucked under the table when not in use.

+ Try using a different wall colour or finish as an alternative way to visually zone a dining spot. Wallpaper that features colours used elsewhere in the space can instantly create a different vibe, or for something subtler, try adding tongue and groove panelling around the seating area only, to create a booth-style diner vibe.

+ Go super bold and pair a dark inky tone with a vibrant red. For a recent project with Soho House 76 Dean Street, an opulent London members club, I opted to colour drench the space in deep Teal 03, then used vibrant Red 03 for their bar (both in eggshell finish). It looked incredible, and would easily translate into a home dining space to give it a going-out-out feel at home.

The warm yellow undertones in Green 05 really help stop this north-facing room feeling gloomy. Adding shaker-style peg rails to kitchen and dining room walls is a clever way of sneaking in extra storage.

Mixing different styles of furniture helps make a traditional dining room feel less formal. This midcentury dining set ties in with the warmth of Blue 03 on the walls, while contrasting with the fireplace and cornicing.

Laura's mixed-use kitchen/dining area is a great example of a homely dining space, which feels more like a living room than a kitchen thanks to its open shelving, vintage furniture and abundant houseplants.

West-facing dining rooms can feel really cosy and magical when those late afternoon and evening rays hit them, helping to warm up beige and green tones.

Primary bedrooms

As the most private space in the house, the bedroom offers a lovely opportunity to inject your personality and create an intimate space that's just for you (and your sleep partner, if you're cohabiting). It's often the first room we're able to decorate exactly as we'd like, whether (like me) that was your parents giving you free rein in your childhood bedroom, or renting your first room in a house-share. I still feel that same sense of freedom and possibility when decorating bedrooms, whether it's for a client or myself.

You'll obviously be using this room at night, but factor in how you'll experience daylight in here, too. I'm an early riser and love waking up to sunlight streaming in, so have always opted for light colours in my own bedroom. But if you're more of a night owl and prefer to stay up (and sleep in) later, then scrumptious darker, deeper colours might suit you better and offer a cosier feel. And if you're a light sleeper (or just love a restorative daytime nap), blackout curtains or blinds would be well worth incorporating, so you're not disturbed by bright daylight when you're trying to doze.

Good sleep is incredibly important, so whatever style you choose, you'll want this space to feel very calm. As with living rooms, colour drenching can be a great way to achieve this, because it visually hides the transitions between walls, ceilings and woodwork, meaning there's less contrast to draw and distract the eye. And as a space you'll be lying down in for much of the time, reducing these contrasts can be even more beneficial, helping the space flow together beautifully and encourage rest.

Try this:

+ Loft bedrooms usually have irregular sloping ceilings and limited head height. I'd always advise taking a colour drenching approach here too, instead of inadvertently highlighting those awkward corners or funny little patches of ceiling with a bright white paint. Softening these with one wraparound colour will allow your bed to become the focal point, instead.

+ If you're decorating a guest bedroom rather than your own, while this still wants to feel calming and relaxing, it can also give you the opportunity to be a tiny bit more adventurous and play with colour and pattern slightly out of your comfort zone. This could mean stepping into the dark side, trying out a wallpaper, or adding contrasting colour in accent areas for a slightly bolder look that won't stop guests from getting a good night's sleep.

@elizabethstanhope; walls and ceiling in White 03, woodwork in Yellow 02

This muted warm pink helps liven up the potentially dull light in a north-facing bedroom. While a red would be too stimulating for a sleep space, knocked-back pink offers a nurturing alternative.

Warm yellow screams sunshine and, used in an east-facing bedroom, is a perfect option for early birds. Pairing it with a warm white with yellow undertones creates a far softer contrast than a pure white.

@chlohannant; walls in Taupe 03

While this grey-toned pale blue could feel chilly in a north-facing bedroom, here it feels welcoming thanks to the warmer daylight it receives. These lighter tones can help our minds to switch off.

Taupe can be a great all-round colour for bedrooms, offering visual warmth and bringing a nurturing feel. It's equally at home with nature-inspired blues and greens, or with flashier pops of red.

Children's bedrooms and nurseries

Whether you're preparing a nursery for the arrival of a new baby or helping your teen redesign their bedroom to reflect their swiftly evolving identity, decorating a child's space is a fabulous opportunity to have some fun and embrace your own inner child, too. In fact, on client consultations these are often my most-asked questions – all parents want their child to love their room, but feel daunted by what approach to take, especially if their little ones are prone to changing their minds at a moment's notice.

I always encourage matching your child's energy and enthusiasm, letting their imagination run completely wild, before refining their fantastical ideas into practical designs (without necessarily installing a life-sized spaceship in the middle of their room). Instead, look at ways to incorporate their desires on a more decorative level: for example, cladding lower walls with wooden panelling and painting on circular 'portholes' (with sky blue paint on upper walls and ceiling) to create a 'pirate ship', which would be easy to paint out when their tastes change. If they're crazy about a particular cartoon character and desperate for that to form part of their design, bring them in through easily-removable elements, such as themed duvet sets or wall decal stickers.

Paint is one of the easiest and most inexpensive ways to radically transform a room, and for children's rooms especially, I love to add some interest by including simple painted patterns. For example, you could use two different colours on the upper and lower halves of walls, but define the split with a scalloped or semi-circle edge rather than a straight line; or add chunky stripes across the ceiling and walls to create a circus tent look. These techniques can look striking and don't require any artistic skill, just a bit of measuring and masking (I've shared some how-to steps for achieving both these effects on page 216). And if you're keen for their room to feel like it shares a similar aesthetic to the rest of the house, look at ways you can bring in relevant touches through the specific tones or materials you choose, to keep you both happy.

Try this:

+ If you're unsure how to combine lots of different (and potentially bright) colours into one room, refer back to the double- and split-complementary and dyadic and triadic colour wheel relationships on pages 36–39, which give you an easy framework to follow and adapt.

+ Containing statement colours to furniture or woodwork trims can make them easier to change than repainting entire walls (especially for freestanding pieces, which you can simply remove from the room and repaint elsewhere).

+ If you really don't like bold hues but your child is nagging for some colour, try using them in 'hidden' spaces instead, for a fun element of surprise. For example, opt for baby blue-painted wardrobes, but paint the insides in fire engine red: trust me, your little one will love it!

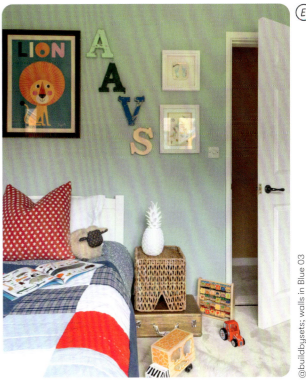

@buildbysets; walls in Blue 03

A predominantly green colour scheme and a design heavily based on nature creates a soothing, grounding look and feel.

Containing pops of more stimulating colours like bright red as accents in cushions and bedlinen means they won't be in your little one's eyeline as they're nodding off to sleep.

@kidofthevillage; lower walls in White 05; upper walls White 01

Neutral tones can create a soothing feel for younger children's sleep and play spaces. Panelling lower walls and painting them in an eggshell finish is practical, too, giving them a toddler-height, wipe-clean finish.

Both paint colours used here have yellow undertones in their mix, and by pairing them with this golden-toned duvet cover they're really pulled out despite their colour being relatively neutral, creating a warm look.

Primary bathrooms, en suites and downstairs cloakrooms

Bathrooms are often the smallest room in the house, whether yours is shared by the rest of your household or you have the luxury of a private en suite or additional downstairs cloakroom.

For a primary bathroom or en suite, I always think a calm, serene, spa-like feel is the way to go, especially if yours has a bath to languish in as well as a shower for everyday use. Too much visual drama in a small space will counteract those relaxing vibes, so I usually recommend a colour drenching approach here, to make it feel a little cosier and more united.

When renovating, choose your tiles first as they'll be the star of the show (along with your main fixtures and fittings), then you can base your exact choice of paint colours and accessories around them. To counterbalance the cold, reflective surfaces and bright white sinks and toilets found in most bathrooms, opt for lower sheen tiles, or go for a brushed finish on taps and shower heads in warm metals instead of high-shine cool chrome. Coloured sinks and toilets have become far more popular in recent years, and certainly make a style statement.

Downstairs cloakrooms or WCs tend to be teeny-tiny and dimly lit, containing little more than a toilet and sink. Your instinct here might be to play it safe with white or light tones, but I really encourage you to take the opposite approach and go all-out, bringing in dramatic colours or bold wallpapers to blur boundaries and absorb shadows. This actually creates the illusion of more space, as your eyes have somewhere to go. This isn't a room you'll be spending much time in, so why not make it fun and dynamic instead of neutral and a bit meh?

Try this:

+ Refresh the look of basic white tiles by bringing in a coloured grout: dark grey makes them look instantly chic (and hides the dirt), while an unexpected bright can create a more retro, graphic look. Grout pens are a great low-effort DIY option to add colour to existing grout.

+ A classic interior designer's trick is to choose wall-mounted sinks, toilets and cabinets in a small bathroom space: the more floor you can see, the larger the room will feel.

+ Plain coloured tiles can be a great way to add in pattern: try creating a chequerboard look with alternating tones, or go graphic and add in the odd contrasting colour to create a subtle yet unusual look across a tiled wall.

If your bathroom lacks character, a simple panelled wall can be transformative in areas away from direct water, and can also be used to hide pipes and create a seamless look.

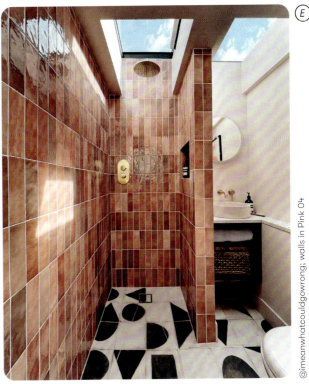

@imeanwhatcouldgowrong; walls in Pink 04

I love the drama of Nathalie's loft shower room, with its bold pink tiles really coming to life when the direct morning sun streams through her roof lights, creating an immersive tonal look alongside the pink walls.

Half-height tongue and groove panelling is a great way to add period charm to a WC, and works in place of tiles (though I'd recommend an eggshell finish, for durability).

@designinglilyspad; room colour drenched in Taupe 03   Photo: @amiecharlot

Colour drenching can work especially well in bathrooms, helping to create a cosy, cocooning feel – here, Lily has artfully used tiles and a vanity unit in similar tones, to enhance the effect.

Home office spaces

This decade has seen a huge growth in working from home, whether flexi- or full-time. And although we don't all have the luxury of a dedicated study, it's important for both productivity and mental health to try and carve out a fit-for-purpose space to accommodate this, even if it's by commandeering a corner in a multi-use guest bedroom/home gym/laundry drying spot. Working from home also enables you to personalise your environment so it better suits your needs and tastes and feels like a natural extension of your home (rather than inadvertently recreating a sterile corporate office aesthetic).

A home workspace needs a careful balance of restfulness (so it's not accidentally spiking your stress levels) and stimulation (to help you get 'in the zone' and inspire innovative ideas). Green is often my go-to here, as its balanced nature means your eyes don't have to put any effort into adjusting to it (which gives our brain one less thing to think about). Its wide palette provides a choice of colours to play with, from warmer yellow-toned greens to blue-based teals, which are also versatile enough to suit the potential other uses of this space.

I'd suggest going slightly bolder here with mid-tones over light neutrals. Test out some richer colours, or play with saturation levels to find your best fit. Use bolder colours strategically, too: if you're spending lots of time in video calls, try a more vibrant tone on the wall behind your desk and go a little lighter in the rest of the room (not to impress colleagues with your good taste, but so you can effectively switch this brighter tone on and off, rather than looking at it directly all day). A bolder painted ceiling can offer a similar hit, and you could even bring its colour down across the upper third of your walls to contrast with gentler, soothing tones on the rest of the walls, to provide balance.

Try this:

+ Great storage is key if this space needs to switch roles regularly. Where possible add in a mix of open shelving and closed cupboards, so you can keep your gym weights and spare linens out of sight and mind when you're trying to work.

+ Pattern helps bring interest and personality into a home office. I'd avoid wraparound wallpaper with loud patterns though; bring pattern in more subtly through interesting art and soft furnishings instead.

+ If this room incorporates a bed (whether it's a guest room or you're working in a corner of your bedroom), try to zone yourself off from this in whichever way is most practical. For a guest room, placing the bed lengthways against a wall can help transform it into a daybed, or simply use a foldable room divider to zone yourself off from your bedroom background while you work.

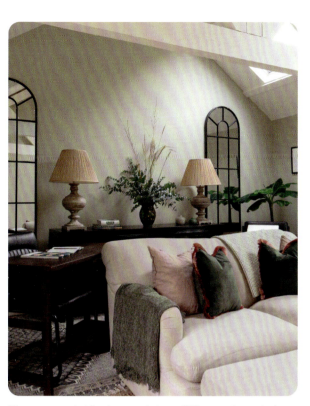

Who says your desk has to go against a wall? If space allows, placing it more centrally in the room – or at an angle – can help to create a zoned effect.

@jimchapman; walls in Green 04

Green 04 works really well in a study, as it brings the thought-provoking benefits of green, while its strong blue undertone means it's mentally stimulating - perfect both at your desk or in a 'breakout area'.

The direct south-facing light this room receives really pulls out the blue undertones in Black 01, giving it an almost teal look (beautifully balanced with a light, warm pink).

@53houseplantsandme; walls in Green 0 , ceiling in White 03

Build on a green theme with complementary rustic wood surfaces and wooden wall cladding, to link to the outside. While the look is soothing, the warm yellow paint tones and wooden surfaces creates a cosy feel.

3

Investigate:
assess your practicalities and restrictions

In the last Perfect Palette exercise (pages 82–83), we looked more broadly at your personal tastes, styles and influences – now, we're getting down to the specifics. This exercise is more of a fact-finding mission (for the odd questions that are more emotive, try to keep the same objective approach).

This two-part checklist covers both general information about your home as a whole – which you can refer back to for any future decorating projects – then focuses on a specific room you're planning to decorate. If you've got more than one project on the go, fill this part in separately for each space.

Remember, you can jot your answers down in a notebook, or download a PDF of this page by scanning our QR code and filling it in on your computer or printing it out.

Your home

+ What type of property do you live in? Is it a Victorian townhouse? Or a modern apartment?

+ How much work are you willing and able to do to improve your current home? Do you own it and would ideally like to undertake some major renovations? Or are you renting, or only able to make fairly low-budget, superficial changes? Be realistic: if you'd love to extend your kitchen and add a loft extension but your budget is more lemonade than champagne, it'd be wiser to concentrate on ways to make the existing layout work better.

+ What are the main things you love about your property? It could be its open-plan layout, the views from your back windows, or perhaps its high ceilings.

+ And what don't you love about it? Stick to specific elements, regardless of whether you can change them or not, such as an awkward downstairs layout, a lack of natural light, or limited storage space.

+ How comfortable are you with colour, pattern and 'stuff'? Do you prefer clutter-free clean lines or personality-packed walls and surfaces?

+ If money was no object, what changes would you make to your home? I'd encourage you to let your imagination run wild here – the point is to get those creative juices flowing to see if they produce any genius ideas you could potentially find a way to incorporate.

+ Overall, how do you want your home to make you feel? Do you want it to feel uplifting, fun and social? Or calming, chilled and quiet?

Your project (the room you're planning to decorate)

+ What's the primary purpose or function of your room, and how else might it be used? For example, if you're redecorating your living room, this might be used for watching TV, socialising with guests, working from home, as a children's play area or occasional guest bedroom.

+ What's the orientation of this room, and are there any other elements that affect the light coming in? Maybe it's south facing, but a large tree outside the window tends to block the afternoon sun.

+ Which times of the day do you use this room currently? Are you hoping or planning to change this? This will help you to determine certain practical needs: do you avoid this room during the day as it feels gloomy, or can't relax here in the evening as the lighting is too bright?

+ What do you love about the room's bare bones or architectural features? Perhaps it has a lovely original fireplace, or its square footprint makes it versatile for different furniture layouts.

+ And what don't you love? There might be no obvious focal point, or the positioning of the door and window makes the layout awkward.

+ Which fixed elements are staying (such as flooring, radiators, a boiler or exposed pipes)? Write them down in a list, objectively noting whether you're happy with them or would prefer to hide or disguise them somehow.

+ What added elements (like furniture, rugs or artwork) are you planning to keep in this room? Again, write them all down and note whether they are staying through choice, or through gritted teeth (e.g. you can't afford to replace the sofa; the dining table belongs to your landlord so has to stay). If there are some superficial improvements you could make, such as covering the sofa with a new throw, write that down, too.

+ How do you want this room to ultimately feel? List this out if it's a multi-functional space (for example, you might want it to feel cosy and calming in the evenings, and welcoming and fun during the day).

Katie and Byron's dilapidated 1960s bungalow-turned-modern-farmhouse country home

Katie and Byron took a huge leap of faith when they left their London life behind, baby in tow, to turn a rundown bungalow (and its two barns) into their dream home. But having embarked on such an epic redesign, by the time it came to finishing off the space, they felt overwhelmed with decision fatigue (which is common towards the end of a big project). They were also struggling to find a balance between their conflicting styles (Byron likes quite strong colours whereas Katie favours neutrals).

I was really pleased that rather than plumping for pure white as a way of avoiding making any real choices, they turned to me instead. With my fresh eyes, I had more than enough insight and enthusiasm to help them find their perfect palette, in a way that did justice to the incredible home they'd already created. Katie had a clear idea of how she wanted the home to feel, but couldn't work out what colours (and their combinations) would actually achieve this. She also wanted to reflect the country character of the area, but felt conscious that the bare bones of their home were fairly featureless.

I suggested using colour to bridge the three converted buildings and ensure the entire space flowed and felt like one home telling one story. To create a nature-inspired biophilic feel, which would connect the interiors to the beautiful countryside all around them (something they were very keen on), we quickly landed on a palette of pinks and greens as the perfect foundational colours. By playing with lighter pinks and bolder greens, we were able to include tones they both loved.

The scene is set from the moment you enter their house, where Lick's gorgeous Botanical 03 wallpaper envelopes the walls and ceilings of the entryway, instantly immersing you in this nature-

WHO LIVES HERE?

Katie Tillard Sharp, a beauty-turned-sustainability consultant, husband Byron, a property developer, and their two children Alex and Izzy.

INSTAGRAM

@buildbysets

THE PROPERTY

A dilapidated 1960s bungalow with a radical revamp. Their U-shaped home's entrance opens directly into the home's heart – an open-plan kitchen and living space. The former barns are now fully incorporated into the home, and also house a dining room, playroom, office, five bedrooms, three bathrooms (two en suite) plus a utility and boot room space leading onto the garden.

PREFERRED COLOURS AND STYLES

Elevated country-luxe with a family friendly feel that reflects the natural environment it sits in.

inspired concept and giving you a flavour of what's to come. From there, a range of green and pink tones across paint, furniture, art and accessories all help continue this story, alongside layers of natural textures and materials, from wooden furniture, linen upholstery and jute rugs to natural stone worktops and surfaces.

To zone Katie and Byron's generous open-plan kitchen and living room, and create the country-luxe look they wanted, we chose dark hunter green shaker-style cabinets (which makes their antique brass handles really pop and complements the Pink 02 walls to perfection), while the sitting area was kept a little lighter and brighter, switching to green accents such as soft furnishings and plants. This allows their stunning 'artwork' (which is actually two framed wallpaper panels – SUCH a clever idea) to sit really harmoniously within the space while still acting as its focal point.

Green 06 was then continued as a woodwork trim in their dining room (and taken across the picture window frame too, to lead the eye outside). With a monochromatic colour approach, the walls were treated tonally with lighter Green 01. Across their three bathrooms, similar tones are picked up across metro tiles and vanity units. The scheme was softened in their main bedroom, this time with a monochromatic paint palette of Pink 01 on the walls and Pink 02 on woodwork for a nurturing feel, with greens coming through as furniture accents instead.

This darker green and soft pink combo pops up again in their utility area and boot room, too: I always think it's important to show a little love

to these hard-working, back-of-house spaces as they're often where we spend a lot of time (or pass through regularly). The effort here was really worth it, where the addition of tongue and groove wall panelling gives instant character and looks absolutely stunning in vibrant Green 07 (and its eggshell finish really helps it pop). I've never been more envious of a humble coat storage area!

Katie's core house palette

KEY PARENT COLOURS

KEY PARENT COLOURS

LEADING LICK PAINT PICKS

| PINK 01 | PINK 02 | GREIGE 02 | GREEN 01 | GREEN 06 | GREEN 07 |

'Byron and I were really feeling the pressure from the amount of colour choices we had to make (and knew it could hold up pulling our home together if we kept procrastinating over it). But once we'd figured out what our key colours were going to be, it was surprisingly easy to create our finalised paint palette, and tie it in with our other design choices. We'd worked so hard to build this house, seeing it all come together – and experiencing how well it connected to our surroundings – was incredibly satisfying, and a huge relief.'

– K A T I E –

Combining colours and using paint strategically

So far, we've looked at the properties of colours in isolation – as well as how you might combine them using the colour wheel – but the real magic comes when we look at colours holistically as part of an overall palette. Now we're going to get into the juicy stuff and dive into how you can actually pull together your own perfect palette with confidence and ease.

Having worked on over 5,000 colour consultations (and counting!) I've organically created my own process to work out not only which individual colours pair well together, but also how I can choose the perfect schemes based on my clients' homes, styles and personalities. That's the framework I want to share with you in this chapter, so you feel empowered to complete a colour consultation with yourself (and other members of your household) to determine the exact hues to meet your needs.

Most of us have experienced colour paralysis when faced with a sea of paint swatches, alongside that anxiety-inducing feeling when your excitement

4

about redecorating your home tips into overwhelm. Too much choice often leads to choosing a pure white or neutral scheme as a default, or the bold paint colour or wallpaper you really love ends up relegated to an accent rather than leading your look. I'm not knocking either approach; a well-planned neutral scheme can look absolutely stunning, as can a clever feature wall or accent area, but if you're choosing your colours from a place of fear, and they're not what your heart truly desires, you may have missed out on the opportunity to create your dream scheme.

I deliberately think of this process as a framework rather than 'rules', because often the magic happens when we put the swatches down and allow ourselves to bring in something that doesn't necessarily fit neatly into a planned scheme, but just looking at it brings joy. My aim is to help you find this balance so your home feels curated, but also still like YOUR home – which is ultimately only something you can do.

How to combine colours

We never see one single colour in isolation, whether at home or in nature, and when we're decorating, we need to factor in all the colours in a space – from furniture and flooring to paint and wallpaper. This means taking a 360-degree approach to ensure you're not overlooking key spots like ceilings, or those all-important finishing touches, such as cushions or ornaments.

Trying to factor this in while also choosing paint colours can often feel daunting – but over the course of my 5,000 colour consultations, I've developed my own formula that works for everyone, whatever your style, space or budget – and my clients who lack colour confidence find this super useful. It's simply: stick to a maximum of three key colour hues for each room you're decorating, and five for your whole home. That's it! Well, okay, there's a bit more to it than that. By 'key colours', I'm referring to the 12 hues of the colour wheel (aka the parent colours) – but it also includes the family of each hue, giving you loads of tints, tones and shades containing that key colour to form your overall palette.

And as black, white and grey (the neutrals) aren't classed as hues, you can use these in addition to the key colours. Usually, I suggest choosing complementary neutrals – that's blacks, whites and greys with a dash of other colours in their mix, rather than in their pure form – so they sit more sympathetically with your palette. This approach offers a failsafe structure for creating a scheme that looks polished and chic, whichever colours you choose – and you can trust that everything will work together wonderfully, as long as it relates back to that palette.

Unless you're planning a one-colour monochromatic scheme (which uses tonal variations of just one key hue), I'd recommend referring back to the colour wheel to help you choose which hues to build your two- or three-colour combinations around (check out chapter one, if you need to refresh your memory). And if you're more colour confident and want to try a more complex four-colour scheme, absolutely go for it: I'd recommend a tetradic approach (also discussed in chapter one), just to give you a bit of a steer.

Three ways to choose a cohesive colour palette

+ Consider weight and saturation: sticking with all-light, low-saturation tones will feel soothing and offer little contrast, while darker and high-saturation tones will be bold, bright and stimulating. Mixing in mid-tones – or playing with both ends of the scale – will bring balance and interest.

+ Decide on warm or cool-toned hues: your room orientation will lead the way here. If you want to lead your scheme with a dominant blue, choosing one with a grey undertone will make the room feel cooler, whereas opting for blue with a yellow undertone will help warm up the space. To create more contrast, you could bring in a warm-toned accent colour into a predominantly cool-toned scheme, or vice versa (through furnishings or accessories, as well as paint).

+ Combine paint colours that share the same undertones: this approach is a quick win, ensuring your colours will all sit beautifully together – and can be applied to both a single-room palette or a whole-home scheme.

Create a simple scheme using one, two or three key colours

The colour combinations opposite show how a palette based on just one key hue (in this instance, green) can still offer a wide range of individual colours and moods. Building this out with a second or third hue (here, we've picked blue and orange) broadens the scope, but shows how you can create both high and low contrast schemes however many hues you include. You could bring in many more individual colours from these hues with paint, furnishings and accessories.

Green tonal palettes

GREEN 01

GREEN 19

GREEN 06

WHITE 03

GREEN 13

TEAL 05

With their shared yellow undertones, these earthy greens have a warm feel that evokes a walk in the woods.

Green 13 also contains yellow undertones, but its appearance is on the fresher, zingier side, with Teal 05 leaning more towards blue than brown.

Green and blue dyadic palettes

BLUE 04

BLUE 07

GREEN 07

GREEN 19

TEAL 04

BLUE 02

Blue 07 and Green 07 both pack a punch, with their heavy saturation. Bringing in soothing Blue 04 balances this out.

Mixing fresh and earthy tones together can look really impactful – here, woody Green 19 is back but this time it's contrasted against a fresh teal and cool icy blue.

Green, blue and orange split-complementary palettes

ORANGE 01

GREEN 13

BLUE 04

BEIGE 10

TEAL 04

BLUE 07

Punchy Orange 01 really dials up the drama when teamed with cool, fresh blue and green tones (use it as an accent or on a feature wall to create a statement talking point).

Keeping Blue 07 as the only deep, saturated shade – and placing it alongside warm Beige 10 and fresh Teal 04 – creates an intriguing, easy-to-live-with colour combination.

Create balance

Creating the perfect balance and ratio of colours is just as important within a scheme as the colours you choose. To help with this, I generally advise following the 60/30/10 approach, which is often used by both designers and artists to help create a sense of interest and harmony. Here's how it works:

Playing with colour ratios: three ways

Here's an example to show precisely how this might work, using a green/pink complementary palette of White 06, Pink 02 and Green 07. By playing with the percentage you use these across this 60/30/10% split, you can see how varying these would produce a very different look and feel. (Of course your whole-room palette would include many more tints, tones and shades based on the key hues of pink and green that lead this scheme.)

WHITE 06   PINK 02   GREEN 07

Percentage	Represents	Where to use it	Approach to take
60%	The dominant colour (or colour family) within your space, due to it visually taking up the bulk of your room (even if it's a light or neutral tone).	This usually makes up larger surface areas like walls, floors and ceilings.	Think of this as the strong and stable backdrop to the rest of your scheme – it commonly has a softness to it, which allows you to layer other colours into the mix to lift the whole look.
30%	The sub-dominant or secondary colour/colour family within your space. It'll cover less surface space, but still around a third of the overall room.	This could be your wall or ceiling colour depending on how you're decorating, but often it comes in via bigger furniture pieces and upholstery, such as a sofa, large floor rug or window treatments.	While this would usually complement your dominant colour, it also wants to bring a little more interest to the table – perhaps with a stronger tone, or by bringing in a pattern.
10%	The accent colour (family) in your room. This is like the all-important garnish or seasoning on your dinner: it's a final flourish, but without it the entire dish would be a bit bland.	While it could come in as a contrasting colour on woodwork, often it's in a mix of smaller touches – say, an armchair or side table – but then this same palette is picked up in an amazing piece of art or a statement accessory.	This is a great way to bring in some vibrant, high-saturation colours if you don't want the rest of the room to feel too strong, but it can also be a great way to add a black or dark accent, too.

Two approaches to 60/30/10 colour balancing

This two-colour complementary pink and green palette takes a rich, tonal approach, incorporating various tints, tones and shades while adding in a few cheeky contrasts.

60% The pretty coral hue on the walls and (one) sofa cushion is bold but mid-toned, with an earthy warmth allowing it to work as the dominant colour without feeling overpowering. The warm beige used on the sofa, flooring and wicker storage baskets represents a lighter version of this pink family.

30% While the footstool and sofa cushions take on a lighter tone, there are darker bottle green pops from the plants and accessories.

10% Smaller accents of blues and reds across books, toys and ornaments aren't technically part of this complementary two-colour palette, but they add a little contrast and vibrancy and lift the overall look. They work as they're both analogous to the dominant pink and subdominant green.

This three-colour split-complementary palette is a little tighter, and it's easier to tell at a glance which colour families this palette is based on.

60% The walls here are an off-white which contains a strong yellow undertone, creating a harmonious backdrop for this bolder yellow armchair.

30% As there are less variations of green here compared to its neighbouring image, visually this mid-toned pistachio appears more obvious as the subdominant colour in the space, with plants providing a second dark green shade.

10% The warm, dusky tone used to tile the fireplace is reflected in the armchair cushion and within the artwork on the chimney breast.

@sharnshouse; ceiling and upper walls in Green 03

Create flow across the whole home

We often overlook how our colour and design choices impact the feel and flow of our homes, especially if you're decorating room by room. So when I'm helping clients choose a colour scheme, I always encourage taking a 'red thread' approach. This isn't about a literal thread (or the colour red, either): instead, it's a uniting factor that weaves together different elements of the same story, to help visually connect each room together from the moment you walk through the door.

Although anything can form this red thread, such as a pattern or a particular material, I find choosing one key colour hue as the lead is the simplest and most effective method. Often, it almost chooses itself: on consultations, I always start by asking my clients what their favourite colour is and why, but it's usually already cropping up in multiple areas (we're naturally drawn to colours we associate with a happy memory or positive emotion, even if it's subconscious). From there, we can plan how to incorporate this hue across the whole home – in its many tints, tones and shades – through paint, materials, furniture and accessories.

Building a whole-home palette

Once you've nailed your red-thread colour hue, it's time to build this out into a full palette (which is something I LOVE doing!) So similar to the idea of using up to three key hues for a single room, I generally advise a total of 3–5 key hues for a whole-home palette (including your red-thread hue, but if you're more colour confident, or have a large property, feel free to add more!) And within this, I'd recommend choosing no more than 6–8 individual paint colours which relate to these parent hues, to help create that flow and harmony with ease.

While this might sound restrictive, remember the same colour of pigment-rich paint can look very different between rooms, depending on the natural light each space receives and what else you pair it with. And a complementary neutral, whether light or dark (or a pure black or pure white) would count additionally to your key hues.

Playing with different colour ratios, following the 60/30/10 colour balancing approach over the whole property, will also create a far more varied look, giving you plenty of scope to mix and match in dozens of different individual colours through furniture, art and accessories, too. Trust me, this is a foolproof way to simplify your colour decision-making while still achieving an interesting end result.

Tip

If you've already decorated most of your home and want to improve its flow, look at simple ways you could create cohesion. Adding accessories is an easy and affordable way to introduce unifying colours or materials, while using leftover paint on a small accent area – like a door, or contrasting woodwork – is a low-fuss way to bring in colours from elsewhere.

Insight

What I tend to find when a client's room looks disjointed is that they had a change of heart halfway through; this is usually due to losing confidence and scaling back their plans, or making a late addition to the scheme without factoring in how it sits within the overall balance. Both approaches can result in an unfinished look, which seems to tell two different stories.

That's not to say you can't change your mind, but if you do deviate from your plan – or you're halfway through and something still doesn't feel right – take an objective step back and consider what impact making these changes might have, then adjust other areas accordingly to make sure it all works, rather than defaulting to safer choices.

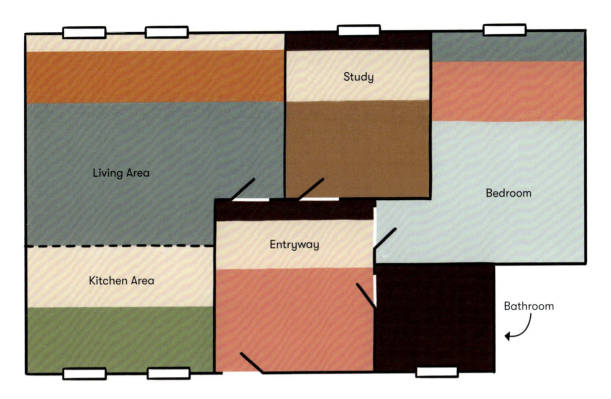

A cohesive colour story in action

Here's an example of a warm, welcoming palette (which also brings in some earthy-toned blues and greens) set in a contemporary apartment, to show you how this works in principle. Its four key hues (red, orange, blue and green) influenced the choice of these eight paint colour picks, with Taupe 03 acting as the complementary neutral for this scheme.

Their placement indicates how you could use them proportionally in each room to create a continuous colour story across the whole apartment. You could then build on this by bringing in other tones of reds, oranges, blues and greens (from the lightest tints to the darkest tones or shades – including colours which share those undertones, such as pinks and browns) through furniture and accessories, to more depth.

You could even switch out certain paint colours altogether: for example, removing Orange 02 from the living room and bringing that hue in with an orange rug or sofa, instead. In certain spots, you might prefer to use just one or two colours rather than three.

Red itself forms the red thread across this apartment, in terms of colour: each room contains tones of red, from subtle warm beige to deep purple, to create that feeling of unity and flow. Think of it like a toolbox, containing everything you need to create your perfect look.

Visually alter the proportions of a room

One of the reasons I love working with colour is because it has almost miraculous properties, and using it strategically to highlight the features we love and distract from those we don't is a great example of this. If you're not able to alter the structure of a tricky room, you can at least use colour to make the space appear more balanced than it really is.

Over the next few pages I'll share some of my favourite ways to do this, but to kick us off, let's look at how it can be used to improve your room's overall proportions.

Using colour to correct proportions

While square rooms aren't necessarily 'best', if the proportions of a room feel odd or awkward it can visually distract us or even make us feel uncomfortable. These three illustrations show how using a strong colour strategically on certain walls and using lighter tones elsewhere can trick the eye into perceiving the space as more balanced than it is.

Trick the eye with the right tone

As we discussed in chapter one, warm colours with longer wavelengths (reds, oranges and yellows) appear visually closer and more prominent, while cooler blues and violets visually recede, giving the illusion of spaciousness. Use this to your advantage and make strategic colour choices. So, if you want your large living room to feel cosy, a red ceiling and warm-toned walls could be the way to go, while in a small bedroom with a low ceiling, painting the ceiling pale blue and adding soft white on the walls would give the illusion of height and space.

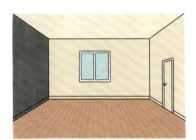

Paint the wall you see when entering the room in a stronger colour, to make an immediate impact (and distract you from any odd proportions). This works better if it's a wall you're not facing all the time (as it can be a little distracting) so is best kept behind, for example, a sofa or bedhead.

In a long room, paint the end wall a stronger colour to visually bring it forward and make the room feel less stretched.

For wider rooms, try painting the two longer walls in a stronger colour than the two shorter ones, which will visually create more of a square shape.

Think outside the box when it comes to using this approach. Elizabeth's hallway has been colour drenched in a light neutral, allowing the bolder downstairs bathroom that leads directly off it to really pop when the door is open, giving depth to this narrow space.

Create a feature area

It's often harder to plan a scheme in rooms with no obvious architectural features, as there's no natural focal point. One way is to create your own, which you can do with both paint (or wallpaper) and furniture positioning. And the good thing is, if you're not restricted by fireplaces or alcoves in potentially awkward places, you've got a little more creative freedom. One of my favourite approaches is to split the wall horizontally: in shorter rooms, I'd do this as a 50/50 split, but for rooms with higher ceilings (and in period properties), I sometimes use the rule of thirds instead. This means using two contrasting colours between the top and bottom half (or top two thirds and lower third) of your walls, to add a talking point that looks chic and modern. And it's really easy to achieve by using masking tape to create this crisp divide when painting (I'll walk you through this in chapter six).

Alternatively, take it vertical by painting colour blocks defined by your contrasting paint colours rather than the corners of rooms and ceilings. This can be a great way to zone areas for different uses, such as a desk space in the corner of a living room, or a dining area in an open-plan living space, as well as to simply create a stunning statement area.

Where to use lighter and darker colours

50/50
Going darker on the lower half (or lower third) of your walls can aid a feeling of space if contrasted with lighter upper walls and ceilings. But in taller rooms, keeping the upper walls dark (with the option of including your ceiling, too) can visually shorten them to create a cosier feel.

Feature nook
Adding a stronger colour to a single wall and continuing it across the ceiling can add drama and also help a narrow room feel wider. You could play with this a little by bringing those lines in to create a zoning, canopy effect within the overall wall and ceiling (this works really well for a bedhead wall). Or get adventurous and define your own area, again using masking tape to keep things neat.

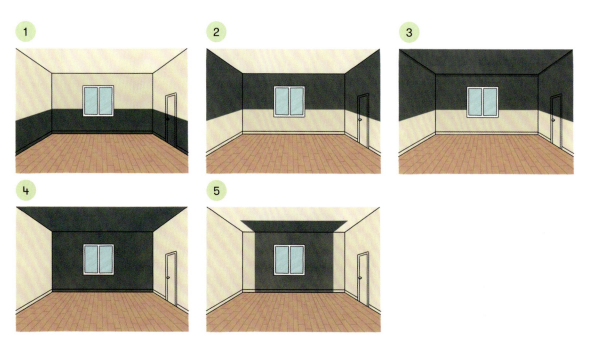

Have a little fun with your feature lines: try incorporating the effect to cut across doors and cupboards, like Jess's bedroom (left), or play with the placement of art or pendant lights to visually break that crisp line, as Emily's done in her dining space (below).

Tip

Going darker on the lower half of a wall is a practical option for high traffic spots, such as a hallway or kid's room, as darker colours will be less likely to show up any dirt. It also means that if you do need to repaint, you don't have to redo the entire walls, just this lower section.

@emilyrickardstyle; lower walls in Green 07, upper walls in White 03

Highlight an architectural feature

There have been lots of articles in recent years stating that the feature wall is 'out', but when it's executed well, it's a wonderful way to highlight any lovely period features or cool built-in elements in a room (and I'd always advocate following your heart over following trends, anyway).

Some of this backlash is because it often ends up as a brightly painted chimney breast or one random contrasting wall that just sort of shouts at you for no apparent reason. It's so important to think about why you're choosing to highlight this area, and how you can tie it in to the rest of the space. But get it right and it can make the whole room sing.

Try this:

+ Always include the sides when you're painting a contrasting colour on protruding elements like a chimney breast – otherwise it can just look like it's floating in mid-air.

+ If your two alcoves are very different in width, painting them both a strong colour with a contrasting chimney breast can highlight this and make the space feel unbalanced. Go for colours with a subtler contrast, or paint the whole area the same colour to highlight it as a whole without drawing attention to these transitions.

+ Where possible I always think it's nicer to keep TVs in alcoves rather than on the chimney breast, so they're not dominating the room, but if yours needs to be here for practical reasons, painting the wall behind it a darker shade will help it to blend in.

Three ways to flag a feature

While the illustrations here focus on a chimney breast and alcoves, the same applies for anything you want to highlight, hide or balance.

Painting the chimney breast a stronger colour can make it stand out, but it can look jarring if the same tone isn't echoed elsewhere. Use the same paint colour on the opposite wall (or two walls either side of it), for balance, or nod to those tones with soft furnishings or decorative accents.

Adding stronger colour to the two alcoves instead can create a more balanced look and help the room feel bigger (as you're not drawing attention to the protruding chimney breast).

For a subtle continuation between your stronger feature colour and the rest of the room, try carrying this strong colour across your skirting boards then leave the rest of your walls and ceilings light.

Alternatively, highlight the whole feature wall by painting the rest of the space (walls and ceilings) darker, then keep this light to draw the eye.

Make sure you definitely want to emphasise the spots you're adding stronger colour to: if your chimney breast is home to a gorgeous fireplace, surrounding it with your feature colour will help highlight it, whereas if it's been previously boxed in, drawing the eye to the alcoves might be preferable.

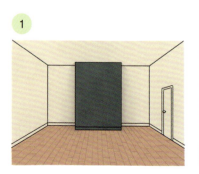

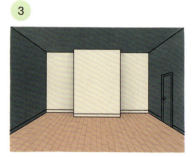

Painting built-in shelving and cupboards creates a united feel and lets their design details (and the books and ornaments you've got on them) become the key focal point.

Incorporate the ceiling into your room scheme

It's so common to overlook the ceiling within a design scheme, which is a real shame – especially when you've gone to all the effort of curating this beautiful pigment-rich palette everywhere else but then painted the ceiling a standard stark white.

Often this is done as we think it'll make the room feel taller and larger (or that it won't command any attention), but what actually happens is your eyes are naturally drawn to it as it ends up being the lightest colour in the room, meaning the rest of your lovely scheme loses its impact. It's important to consider your approach and choose similar or contrasting colours depending on the effect you want to achieve.

If your room has cornicing or crown moulding (the decorative trim which sits between the wall and ceiling, usually found in older properties), factor this in to your strategy, too: make colour choices based on whether you want them to stand out as an accent in their own right, or seamlessly form part of the walls or ceiling.

Three ways to (visually) move a ceiling

 1

High ceilings are generally considered desirable, though they can also make a space feel draughty and cold: counter this by painting them a darker colour (and keeping walls light), which will make the ceiling look lower. This can also work well in modern builds – which tend to have lower ceilings compared to older properties – to create a cosy feel, or add a sense of drama.

 2

Push this further by bringing your darker colour down onto mouldings or even the top third of your walls, too. This is also a great way to add character to a newbuild or featureless space if you've not got any mouldings, as it nods to the idea of having a picture rail.

 3

To draw attention to cornicing, paint it a different colour to both walls and ceilings, whether it's a contrasting tone or just a couple of shades lighter or darker. You could also use the same approach to create a band of colour on the upper third of your walls for visual interest.

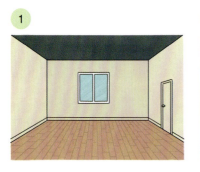

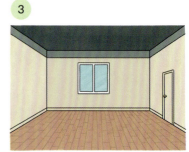

Taking this warm, red-toned ceiling colour down and along the top of Emma's bedroom walls helps soften the warm white used elsewhere, while Jim's dramatic dark teal ceiling highlights his room's generous height and stunning period cornicing.

Tip

For anyone a bit nervous about bringing in colour, painting your ceiling in a bolder complementary tone is a great way to do this without overwhelming the space. It adds a real wow-factor, and even if you go neutral on your walls, you'll still have a statement area. But in rooms with shorter walls, stick to the same (or a tonally similar) colour on both walls and ceilings to avoid drawing attention to the room's shortcomings. And if you do want to go white, opt for a complementary shade to soften this transition (unless pure brilliant white is already part of your scheme).

Hide or highlight woodwork

As with ceilings, woodwork (skirting boards, doors, architraves and window frames) deserves some love and consideration when we're fleshing out a decorating scheme. Woodwork can play a small yet important part in the overall look and feel of a room, making a space feel united.

Think about your overall aesthetic and mood goals for the room, then bring that back to the woodwork: do you want the room to appear larger? What feeling are you trying to evoke? Are you hoping to highlight an accent within the room, or bring in a bit of a designer touch? How could your choice of woodwork treatment help you achieve all this?

Three ways with woodwork

Using a stronger or darker colour on woodwork, then going lighter on walls adds contrast and makes the walls look comparatively lighter. This could be kept to just skirtings, window frames and door trim, or you could paint your door (and cornicing, if you have any) the same colour for a punchier impact.

Light (or white) woodwork is a traditional choice (many of us will have grown up in family homes decorated this way). When paired with light or neutral-toned walls, it creates a low visual contrast and looks stylish and fresh, but check your tones and opt for a complementary white instead of pure brilliant white (unless you're using that elsewhere, too) to avoid its intensity throwing the whole scheme off. Sticking with the same tone on your woodwork, but going a couple of shades darker, looks subtle but incredibly stylish, too.

Applying the same colour to walls and woodwork brings a sense of calm and openness, as there's less contrast. It also makes the room feel taller as the skirting board is effectively blended into the walls. This approach feels contemporary, and I'm seeing more people gravitate towards it as it looks tight and cohesive.

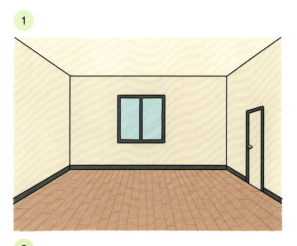

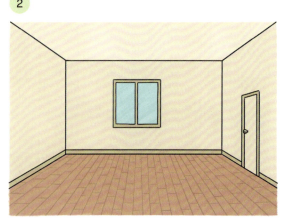

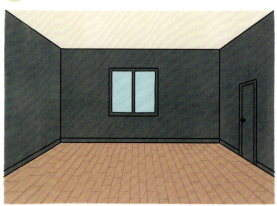

Dark or contrasting paint on feature woodwork, like the spindles of a staircase, can help to highlight its intricate details, while painting the architrave that frames doors the same colour as their surrounding walls draws attention to the rooms and spaces beyond.

Insight

While woodwork was traditionally painted in a highly reflective gloss finish, in recent years (and with paint composition changing drastically to meet environmental standards) it's become possible (and more popular) to use lower sheen finishes. Eggshell is a great way to bring a subtle reflection and a little more durability, while a matt finish can help woodwork blend in more seamlessly against walls.

@kittykellystyle; walls and woodwork in Pink 13. Photo: @daveycleveland

Colour drench a room

You've probably noticed by now that I'm a huge fan of colour drenching, which uses the same paint colour on EVERYTHING (more or less) – from walls and woodwork to ceilings and even the floor (if you've got floorboards, or alternatively you could use a coloured flooring which more or less matches your paint, such as carpet, tiles or coloured vinyl, if you want to take a full 360 approach).

I often find colour-cautious clients are nervous when I suggest this technique, but it's actually an easy look to nail as you're only choosing one paint colour for the entire room. By 'drenching' the whole space in this single colour, you're blurring its lines and hiding a multitude of sins, from reducing the impact of an odd alcove to blending short, stubby walls so the boundaries of the room are harder to make out.

It's a common misconception that you should avoid this approach in smaller spaces or naturally darker rooms, because actually this is where colour drenching can be transformative: with all of those boundaries blurred, all you notice are the gorgeous tones and your lovely décor, rather than low light or tiny proportions.

Light or dark?

Often people assume the term colour drenching ONLY refers to dark or bold colours, whereas in fact it works with any colour, including whites and neutrals (which is an approach I love using in larger, naturally lighter spaces).

Try this:

+ A key benefit of using bolder or darker colours if you're drenching is that it'll show less contrasts. This will make it naturally feel more restful, allowing you to go a bit stronger than you might feel comfortable with on a feature wall.

+ Always include 'ugly' fixtures like radiators when you're colour drenching, painting them out so they disappear into the wall, otherwise you'll be inadvertently highlighting them.

+ When you're mid-way through colour drenching your room, it's common to suddenly feel a bit panicky that it's too full-on, especially if you've gone for a brighter tone. My advice at this stage is to hold your nerve! It will doubtless look very different to how it was before, but trust that once you've added all your furniture and accessories back in, it'll feel far less intense and will look amazing.

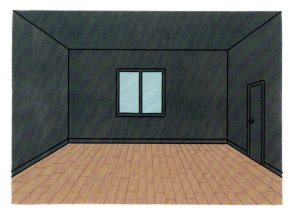

Amira's living room takes the same teal tone used to paint her walls, woodwork and ceiling across her sofa for a cocooning feel. This picks the colour up within the patterns of her rug and curtains, too.

Patterned wallpaper

We've talked a lot about colour in relation to paint, but wallpaper is another excellent way to add colour, texture and pattern to walls (and ceilings too, if you're feeling brave!). It's common to think of wallpaper as a bolder choice than paint, but the design you choose, where you place it and how you integrate it into the rest of the room all play a part.

Introducing patterned wallpaper into a room naturally draws the eye more than a painted wall, as there's more to take in visually. But if you confine that pattern to a single wall or feature area, visually that space will look closer and more prominent, whereas add it to all four walls and the effect is mitigated, as it's no longer a single point of focus.

So if you're considering a feature patterned area but are anxious about it feeling overpowering, I'd actually encourage you to paper all four walls, as this will help create a calmer feel (and make the room look larger, too, as it will blur its boundaries). The key to striking the right balance is making sure there's a harmony or relationship between your wallpapers, paints and any other patterns and textiles in the room.

I've noticed over the past few years that people are becoming braver with their wallpaper choices, just as they have with paint. It seems part of an overall shift to more joyful, personal decorating choices, and this makes me so happy as bringing colour and pattern into our homes is utterly transformative.

Choosing colours to balance your wallpaper

Think about the overall effect you're after here: do you want high drama, or something gentle and tonal? Consider the mood and feel you want to achieve. Obviously, the colours and approach you pick will depend on the design of the wallpaper itself, but here's some general guidance to follow:

For a low-contrast tonal or harmonious look… pick a paint colour that matches or co-ordinates with the dominant colour in your wallpaper: this might be its background, or the largest element within its design. Carrying this across onto neighbouring walls and woodwork will be the best option for blending it in a little more seamlessly.

For a more contrasting or unexpected look… choose a colour that forms an accent or detail within the design, then use that as your main paint colour. This will still sit together visually but offer more interest.

To play around a little more… choose a paint colour that doesn't directly feature in the design but has a tonal relation. So, if your wallpaper features a dark forest green and a sky blue, you could complement this with an analogous pistachio green or contrasting earthy pink paint.

Using wallpaper… in a contained area: features like dado and picture rails (or wall panelling) provide an opportunity to add pattern to just one section of a wall, depending on where you want to draw the eye. In this child's room, both the wallpaper background and surrounding off-white walls and woodwork share a yellow undertone, so adding a bolder yellow to the ceiling brings the look together. This leaf design works in a similar way to a classic striped wallpaper, visually elongating the room and creating the illusion of more square footage.

WHITE 05   YELLOW 02   GREEN 19

Pair it with: White 05, Yellow 02, Green 19

@roisinquinn; walls in Bloombastic 01 Studio Coverdale wallpaper

PINK 01

RED 06

GREEN 06

Using wallpaper... in a bathroom: wallpaper can work wonderfully in 'wet' areas like kitchens and bathrooms – you just need to use a design with a wipeable finish so it's practical in a humid space, and keep it away from areas where it'll come into direct contact with water. I love how Lick's Bloombastic 01 wallpaper takes a traditional floral motif and makes it a bit more contemporary with this colour palette.

Pair it with: Pink 01, Red 06, Green 06

ORANGE 02

BLUE 15

BLUE 07

Using wallpaper... across your ceiling: taking this bold Keeper's Cottage 02 pattern up onto the ceiling as well as on all four walls creates a cocooning effect. Although the pattern is busy, it's also small, meaning the eye passes over it more easily than a larger, graphic design. By keeping everything else in the room neutral and adding a touch of black, the look still feels refined.

Pair it with: Orange 02, Blue 07, Blue 15

A joyful accent

When decorating, it's easy to get bogged down with the big decisions or compare our homes to the perfectly curated images we see on Instagram. But the little touches that bring joy and reflect our personalities are what truly matter. I always tell clients to go ahead and bring in that novelty holiday ornament, or cover their fridge with their kid's drawings, if that's what makes their heart sing and triggers happy memories – that's ALWAYS more important than whether they 'go' with the rest of the space. Every room should have at least one thing in it, however big or small, that makes you smile and tells your story rather than making it feel like a show home.

I often find that helping clients decrease their general clutter allows the room to breathe a little and lets those standout pieces do the talking. I'd never want anyone to feel that something they truly love won't work in their room because it doesn't fit within their colour palette, or its style is too different to the rest of the space. In fact, sometimes it's precisely those pieces which don't work on paper that actually pull the whole space together.

A good way to handle this is to bring in the red thread concept again. If you've decorated your room in tasteful blues and greens, but you've fallen for a maximalist leopard-print vase, absolutely bring it in, but add accents elsewhere that will nod to it, like a couple of neutral cushions with a black and ochre trim on the chair next to it. This approach works for the whole house, too: if you want an all-out maximal room while everywhere else is light and breezy, go for it. Just make sure you use colour to bring through a commonality and soften the transition between the spaces.

Try this:

+ Add a secret splash of colour inside a cupboard or along the edge of a door for some unexpected micro-hits of bold hue throughout the day.

+ Inject surprise fun into a functional area you don't normally spend a lot of time in – such as a downstairs WC, pantry or utility room – to give it some personality.

+ Paint something 'serious' – like an ornate wooden mantelpiece or a Victorian sideboard – in clashing, contemporary tones to change its vibe (painting furniture is also a great alternative to painting walls if you're renting and unable to decorate).

+ Turn exposed wooden stairs into a multi-coloured walkway using leftover paints.

When this door is shut, Mary's bedroom looks relatively calm (aside from the pop of vibrant purple from her floor), but open it up and suddenly this glorious dressing room is revealed, emphasised by the eggshell finish of the deep green paint, which colour drenches the space and bounces light around the room. We also added a chandelier and a leopard-print carpet – because why wouldn't you?!

Light and airy

As you might expect, the colours we perceive as light and airy are often pale and neutral tones with lots of lovely blues, greens and greys – but this needn't mean sticking with cool-toned colours: warmer whites and beiges with pink or yellow undertones can all bring out this easy-breezy feel. These combinations work particularly well in larger spaces with good natural light, and can look lovely in kitchen and dining areas that connect directly to a garden, building flow.

I generally advise sticking to just one white within a room scheme – as they are all so similar, they can sometimes just read as dirtier versions of the same paint. If you want to keep things pale, try using a light grey, greige or taupe, instead.

Insight

Although Lily's's kitchen/diner space is large – and also has high ceilings and a generous window – we wanted to keep things looking light and minimise contrasts, but bring in some warmth, too. To achieve this, we used White 06 to colour drench the walls, ceilings and woodwork, which created a gentle and welcoming feel, perfect for a space that's heavily used throughout the day and into the evening. It also helped to blend in a fitted cupboard in the corner, which is painted in the same tone and almost disappears.

Bringing in darker teal base units added a little more contrast while still linking to this light, warm palette, adding visual interest and making the walls appear lighter. Finally, the addition of warm wooden furniture and some green dining chairs helped the space feel homely and connected to nature.

Two light and airy palettes

Palette One

Leading with White 06 gives you a light, airy scheme. As these colours are all warm, they'd work well in a cooler-toned north- or east-facing space, to help balance this out.

Palette Two

The overall palette here is more balanced, making it a good option for warm-toned south or west-facing spaces. These three colours feel reminiscent of cooler skies.

Cosy and warm

This approach is a really good one to take in rooms that are naturally smaller, or only receive limited daylight. By leaning on colours and patterns with warm undertones, you can achieve a surprisingly transformative effect. These are the spaces where those comforting oranges, pinks and reds can be really good contenders for colour drenching, to wrap that colour all around for a cocooning feel, like you're sitting in a cuddle.

If you're decorating a bedroom, you'll want to avoid going too strong with these tones as they could inadvertently overstimulate you and affect your sleep, but in spaces like a TV room or den you can afford to go a little bit more saturated to really make the most of these comforting properties.

Insight

Frances and Ben really wanted their bedroom to feel cosy, uplifting and serene and with its south-east orientation, it's blessed with lovely warm morning light. This made Pink 03 a perfect option, with its grey undertones ensuring it doesn't feel too sugary-sweet when that stronger sunshine does hit.

The couple REALLY embraced the colour drenching concept here, using it on everything except their floor (where they opted for a plush fitted carpet in a similar tone, to amp up the cosiness and create an almost cocooning feel). Touches of red (in their upholstered headboard and other fabric accents), and the earthy brown of their walnut bedside lamps, both sit tonally with this pink, while touches of complementary forest green in other fabric accents brings the whole room together.

Two cosy and warm palettes

Palette One

Dominant colour

This palette really leans into that nurturing, de-stressing pink tonal scheme, bringing a soothing air. A dash of deep warm purple helps stop this leaning too far towards the sweet side.

Palette Two

Dominant colour

This palette takes an earthier tone, which has a stronger biophilic connection to nature with its beiges and warm green. Green 05 has a heavy yellow pigment, making it feel uplifting and nurturing.

Energising

Creating an energising colour palette usually means bringing in lots of juicy, saturated colour, but that doesn't have to mean going dark – there are lots of mid-toned hues that have a high saturation and bring a dopamine-boosting feeling. Even rich pastel tones could fall into this category if they're on the bolder rather than sugary sweet side.

If you're looking to bring energising tones into rooms used for several purposes, consider keeping them to feature walls or ceilings and balancing the rest of the space with more neutral tones. But for areas where you don't spend huge amounts of time, or which you'd like to give you a mood boost, go for it and colour drench the whole space for a vibrant hit. Pay attention to your furnishings, too: big colour on a wall invites other furnishings to be loud as well.

Insight

Mary fell in love with Green 08, which is a gorgeous fresh, zesty tone, and really wanted to use it in her bathroom. As the room isn't actually that big, and she had already installed some statement black and white chequerboard floor tiles, I suggested we colour drench across the walls (above the tiles), woodwork and ceiling. I felt that a pure or complementary white ceiling would actually look louder and make the space feel disjointed, which was definitely the right call.

This is a great example of how embracing a bolder colour and taking this wraparound approach can look softer than diluting it down with other tones.

Two energising palettes

Palette One

The energising nature of this palette is balanced by the shared tones between dominant Green 08 and subdominant Teal 06, meaning there's not a huge contrast between them. I love this pairing as it's so luscious, and adding a flash of complementary orange gives an uplifting accent. This would look glorious in a hallway.

Palette Two

This palette shows how you can still lead with a neutral in an energising scheme and achieve an impactful result, even if you don't want to use a bold colour as your dominant. White 03 has a lovely yellow undertone, which sits sympathetically with the highly saturated Yellow 03 and Blue 10 accents so they don't feel overpowering.

Dark and moody

Contrary to popular belief, dark colours don't necessarily make rooms feel smaller. In fact, they can bring a feeling of spaciousness to small spaces, making them appear larger and more open, whereas with larger, light-filled rooms it can feel like you're fighting against their nature if you try taking them down the dark and moody route.

Painting small rooms in these luscious deep tones will make those shadows disappear and open up the space while adding a little drama. To push this effect even further, opt for cooler darks and deeper blue tones, which will appear as if they're receding and visually push the space back further. You can also use dark accents to highlight an amazing feature, such as a pretty view from a window, or to make more of a statement of a wooden mantelpiece.

Insight

If you paint a room in a darker colour, but leave the ceiling and woodwork white, the strong contrast can make the room feel shorter and even darker. What Emily has done so beautifully here (see left) is have the confidence to opt for a complementary colour on the ceiling (Red 03), echoed by the colour of the carpet, to make the space feel really designed and considered.

Or you can go for a tonal scheme and choose one to two tones lighter on the ceiling and woodwork to soften the transition from walls to floor and ceiling.

Two dark and moody palettes

Palette One

I regularly use Teal 03 in dark and moody schemes as it's a colour that changes so much throughout the day (and it also looks amazing by candlelight at night). This palette really leans into those blue and green tones; the blue undertone of the teal and green helps them sit well together, then the grey in this pinky-red accent gives it a little lift (and you can never go wrong with pairing green and pink).

Palette Two

Black is really under-used as a dominant paint colour, but it's incredibly versatile. The key to using it across a whole room is to balance it with some slightly lighter, earthy tones. Green 05 looks amazing against Black 02 as they both share a warmth, while Brown 02 shares a red undertone and brings a lighter tonal accent into the mix.

Calm and relaxing

Insight

Spaces that lean into these calm, relaxing vibes can share a similar palette to the light and airy schemes we looked at a few pages back, but for this colour story I tend to reach for a slightly stronger yet still soft set of hues.

The key here is to bring in warm and balanced tones over anything too cool-toned, to aid this relaxed vibe. These are ideal for spaces like living rooms and bedrooms, where you want to feel chilled. The colours I'd suggest here would be those lovely beiges and soft pinks along with tones like greige and sage green. You want less contrast here, so keep things tonal, painting walls and woodwork in the same – or similar – colours.

When recommending colours to evoke a calming feel, I always refer to nature to help create a relaxing environment. For this bedroom, Lucy used Beige 03 on all the walls to create an intimate yet interesting backdrop for the other natural tones in the space. Lucy's beautiful bedroom was ALL about softness, which you can see from the colour palette as well as details like the wavy edge along the top of the headboard and the gentle scalloped and frilled trims on her pillows and cushions. There are no sharp edges in this room, even the hard materials have a softness, from the brushed brass trim on her mirror to the tactile powder finish of her blue table lamp. Tonally everything sits tightly together, which brings a calming, undemanding feel to the room.

Two calm and relaxing palettes

Palette One

| BEIGE 03 | Beige 03 | | Green 02 | Green 09 |

Dominant colour

I love to champion earthy beige palettes – they're sometimes dismissed as being boring whereas, when handled well, they can be so beautiful. This palette leans more heavily towards nature and falls into the neutral side, making it very calming, supportive and balanced.

Palette Two

| TAUPE 03 | Taupe 03 | White 06 | Pink 07 |

Dominant colour

Containing more clay-toned pigments gives this palette a pinky look, which creates a relaxing, warm feeling. Pink 07 brings a more grounding feel and would look beautiful on woodwork or an accent table.

4

Define: firm up your design aims

So far with our Perfect Palette exercises, we've played with colour and looked at how this relates to your personal tastes as well as your practical requirements and restrictions. But before we move onto choosing a colour scheme and creating a moodboard, I'd encourage you to go through one final checklist here, so you know exactly where to focus your thoughts when we get there.

As before, you could write these down on paper or make a note on your phone for easy reference, but you can also scan the QR code on this page to access a printable download to fill in directly.

Some final questions

Fill these in for the room you're planning to decorate: if it's more than one space, answer separately for each.

+ Are there any specific aspects of the room you'd like to highlight (such as a fireplace, or a statement window)?

+ Would you like the room to feel taller/shorter or narrower/wider? Add any ways you'd like to use paint to visually alter the proportions of your space.

+ Is there anything you'd like to hide or gloss over (like an ugly radiator or an awkward alcove)?

+ What about your woodwork: is that something you're keen to feature, or do you want it to just blend in?

+ How colour confident are you feeling? Would you rather stick to a simpler one-colour monochromatic or two-colour dyadic or contrasting palette? Or are you keen to try a three-colour triadic or split-complementary scheme? Or perhaps even attempt a four-colour tetradic look?

+ Are you keen on the idea of bringing in some wallpaper? If so, how do you think you might use it? On one wall, across the whole room or wrapping it up and onto your ceiling as well?

+ Without worrying about colour and pattern choices right now, which way do you think you might head in terms of style direction? Neutral walls with a contrasting ceiling? A dark colour drench? Wallpapered alcoves and a contrasting chimney breast?

We'll talk more about finding inspiration in the next chapter, and I'll lead you through pulling all of this together into a moodboard, but you can write down any thoughts you already have relating to your scheme's starting point now, such as if you have a favourite artwork or statement curtains you'd like to base the room around.

@designinglillyspad; rooom colour drenched in Taupe 03 Photo: @amiecharlot

Create your own style story

We've explored colour theory and looked at many different design approaches, but the most important aspect of creating your perfect space is actually understanding yourself: what do YOU like? Which styles set YOUR heart aflutter and which ones are a firm thank-you-but-that's-not-for-me?

In this chapter, we're going to get hands-on as we play with material swatches, test out some paints and get out and about beyond our homes to find colour and style stories that really light us up. We'll then pull it all together to create a moodboard that distils all of this into one place.

We'll also consider potential design influences (in the broadest sense), exploring how culture, travel, art and nature can capture our imaginations and spark genius design ideas. While it can be helpful to explore different interior design styles and bring them into the mix, I encourage clients to create their own unique look that blends together their favourite styles and influences, rather than simply copy what someone else has created. Imagine if you only looked in one place, which favoured one specific style, for all your inspiration – chances are, that's what your home would end up looking like, too. That's not a criticism, but it's really important we notice when

5

our influences might be blinkered, even if that look IS one that we really love. Looking beyond your bubble can really open you up to new discoveries.

What I want you to take away from this chapter is the knowledge that we're ALL creative, whether you're an artist or an accountant. Often we confuse creativity with being inherently good at something 'artistic', like playing a musical instrument or composing the perfect painting. And yes, some people are naturally gifted in certain areas, but their work is also the result of countless hours spent learning, practising and refining their craft.

Some of us may be more tuned in to our creativity (for example, my dyslexia means I'm more attuned to my visual environment), but everyone has the ability to create a beautiful home with a little guidance. So who better than you to steer these choices? This is why I always say I work with my clients, rather than for them: my job is to help them discover what they truly desire in their homes, then help bring it to life. I can easily create an objectively well-curated interior scheme for someone, but unless they feel connected to it personally, they're never going to love it.

What do you REALLY like?

Over the next few pages, we'll look at how to identify and understand your style (with the emphasis on YOUR). Because, while looking can provide us with inspiration, no one fits neatly into one style box – and why should we? We're all unique, and our homes should reflect OUR story rather than simply mimicking a magazine spread.

In fact, there's been a noticeable shift in recent years towards making our homes into spaces for personal expression. They're often where we spend more time than anywhere else, so why decorate them to impress others when you could turn them into a haven filled with everything you love the most? This might mean proudly bringing in a bright orange retro sofa that reminds you of your grandparents' home, or decorating your modern city-centre apartment with a rural aesthetic to contrast sharply with your surroundings.

Factor in the rest of your household

Many of us share our homes with partners, children, housemates or multiple generations of our family. While this can bring design challenges, finding a common ground allows you to incorporate styles and colours that will please everyone.

Start with a key element everyone's on board with – whether that's a particular design style or a shared favourite place – then build a colour palette around that, incorporating tones that are to everyone's tastes. If your spouse prefers a neutral look but you love bold, bright hues, see if a palette with earthy neutrals (over tinted whites) as the dominant colour and a slightly stronger sub-dominant with a cheeky 10% dash of your favourite complementary bright tone could offer a happy compromise.

Remember, colour itself is subjective: how we perceive and process colour varies between all of us (whether we're more finely attuned to spotting subtle tonal differences or experience colour blindness, meaning certain shades are difficult to make out or appear murky and dull). Our personal preconceptions also play their part: if you're describing a decorating scheme to your spouse as you see it in your mind's eye, they might be imagining something VERY different.

What's your style?

It helps – especially if your head is being turned by the beautiful homes of your favourite influencers – to stay open-minded and discern which elements (such as colours, furniture and layout ideas) you'd genuinely love to bring into your own home, versus what you find objectively beautiful or interesting but know deep down isn't for you. These are often two very different things, and it's easy to mix them up.

Take a good look at the rooms opposite. Consider what makes their designs successful based on the principles we've discussed – do they contain a proportionally balanced range of colours? How have they created a sense of harmony throughout the space? Do you get a sense of each inhabitant's personalities? You can learn a lot just by analysing a well-executed scheme, regardless of whether it aligns with your own tastes and preferences.

@roseashbycooks; room colour drenched in White 03

Nature

Inspiration for colour schemes and decorating ideas can be found literally anywhere, so don't limit yourself to photos of other people's homes. I often find a trip somewhere new is a great time to collect colour inspiration, whether that's an exotic holiday or just a visit to a local park you've not frequented before. These new environments might encourage you to notice unique colour combinations, from the vibrant reds and greens of Morocco's sun-bleached buildings to the complementary colours in your local park's flower beds.

We went through some colour-hunting exercises at the end of chapter two, and I'd love you to take this practice through into your daily life, staying mindful of unexpected flashes of inspiration as you're running errands or watching TV. And when they strike, try recording them as a note (or with a photo), to help you remember what inspired you, and why.

These moments can all help to inform your design concepts, whether that's a specific combination of colours you're loving (say, the warm sunshine tones in the pomegranate salad you're eating), or a more general feeling of airiness and space.

Digital colour-picking tools are a really fun and interesting way to explore the individual tones in an image. Try uploading a photo from your camera roll (or an image found online) into an app like Canva (which has lots of great tools in its free version). Play around by manually picking a mix of colours you love – you might be surprised at the variety. This can help shape the overall colour palette of your project generally, or inform more specific paint and material choices.

Colour combinations

Nature is the ultimate influencer, whether we're talking about the big-nature view of a revered beauty spot or a tiny detail like the contrasting colours in a petal. You simply can't go wrong when using nature to inspire your palette, as these combinations (and ratios) will always look wonderful replicated elsewhere.

There's also a near-limitless variety in nature, too: if a bird of paradise inspired a decorating scheme, it would definitely be a maximal one full of bold, vibrant tones. Even the puffin – with its mainly black and white body – mixes things up with that flash of vibrant orange-red on its beak and feet. If the puffin were a Lick colour scheme, I'm pretty sure it'd be 60% Black 02, 30% White 02 and 10% Orange 01.

@kaytrainillustrator; walls in Grey 02; ceiling in White 03

This fun-yet-tranquil scheme shows how nature can inspire your interiors, both literally and through more abstract and subtle details. Here, the colours from these pretty pebbles are referenced in the room's grey walls, warm neutral furniture and vibrant decorative accents – while its rounded headboard and curved wall lights mimic the organic shapes of them, too.

Equally, a much broader view can form a brilliant basis for a colour scheme: returning to the idea of colour hunting in a local park, its green grass and blue skies could be represented in a 50/50 feature wall, or referenced in a kitchen by painting your base units green and wall units blue. Layering in some related details – such as a rustic wood sideboard to reference the park's trees, or a brushed steel worktop as a nod to the light grey clouds shimmering in the sun – could all help build this style story.

Art, fashion and hospitality

Alongside nature, I often look to art and fashion as well as venues, such as hotels and restaurants to get my creative juices flowing (these are often starting points for my clients, too). Here's how I use them to help inspire a scheme.

Art

Artists instinctively know where, how and in what proportion to use colour in order to draw us in and create an emotional connection. My husband and I are both obsessed with art, and I often base room palettes around favourite pieces. The key to doing this successfully is to avoid being too literal and pull colours out of the art which are tonally related, instead. So say it's a predominantly dark blue seascape, you could pick out a lighter blue as your main wall colour, to relate to it without it looking too matchy-matchy, then use dark blue as an accent in your soft furnishings.

Consider the shapes and patterns in your art, as well as the colours: I based the design of our son's nursery around a beautiful painting that features tiny yellow hot air balloons dotted across the skyline (see page 21). To reference this within his room, I painted a scalloped edge border to divide the upper and lower walls and mimic the shape of these balloons.

Fashion

We're often a little more willing to experiment with pattern and colour combinations in our wardrobes than our homes (a shirt featuring a vibrant print is far cheaper – and less permanent – than using a similar pattern on your sofa or carpet), but if your closet is full of adventurous designs while your home is plain and neutral, you could be missing out on decorating in a way that really brings you joy.

Try adding vibrancy into your home through smaller, flexible accents. Textiles are a great option here, whether that's a bold cushion, colourful throw or even a reversible bedspread, so you can easily switch up these pattern pops. Also consider the relationship between your dress sense and décor. In this bold living room (see right), Alanna's equally bold style perfectly mirrors her overall aesthetic. Whereas if your wardrobe is full of 1950s-style ditsy florals, bringing that vibe into your home might better suit your tastes.

Hospitality

Public spots like hotel lobbies, restaurants and cafés often showcase bolder, more conceptual designs than residential spaces. These are often a key source of inspiration for bedrooms and bathrooms in particular (my clients often mention wanting a 'boutique hotel look' for these spaces).

You might choose to emulate the cosy feel of a gorgeous restaurant you visited on holiday, which glowed under its soft lighting and deep, moody colours. Or maybe the cool industrial-chic café you had brunch in, with its exposed copper pipes and bare plaster walls, could influence your upcoming kitchen renovation. The same applies to tinier touches, like storing neatly stacked towels on open shelves or decanting toiletries into ceramic dispensers to bring that boutique bathroom feel into your own en suite.

What IS a moodboard and why do I need one?

You probably have an idea of what a moodboard is, even if you haven't made one before. But it's a term that sometimes causes confusion, or even anxiety if you're worried about getting it 'wrong'. Over the next few pages I'll walk you through the process so you can use it as it's intended: as a valuable tool to help you nail that perfect-for-you look.

First, let's define exactly what we're talking about here. As you might have guessed from the name, a moodboard is basically a board (or surface of some kind) that contains a mixture of paint and material samples, inspirational images and any other physical references that together evoke the mood and style of your scheme. Things can get a bit sketchy if you jump straight in to choosing exact colours and materials before you've worked out what look and feel you want to create, so this is a really important step.

I'd love you to start off with some image hunting and analysis before committing to specific elements. Keeping your options open at this early stage is super important; if you've already fallen in love with a particular colour swatch or wallpaper pattern, hold onto it – but you might be boxing yourself in if you fix on a rigid idea too soon. Once you're happy with your initial research, we'll start to analyse and refine it so you can confidently choose some samples to test, before creating a really powerful moodboard that will help steer your whole scheme.

Your own moodboards might include images that represent the look and feel of your scheme more literally, or more suggestive elements that hint at the aesthetic. Ultimately, the goal is the same: to offer a snapshot of how your finished space will come together, through finalised material and colour selections and supporting elements which nod to the overall vibe.

Whole house or individual room?

Before we begin, think about whether you want to pull together ideas for your whole home, or a specific room or area. Even if you're only decorating one room right now, it's still really useful to consider how this will tie in with – and affect the flow of – the rest of your home, whether you've recently renovated everywhere else or you're not planning on making any other changes.

Either way, the approach and the process don't really differ, although for a whole-house project it can be helpful to start with a broader concept that relates to your entire home, so you can then use it to feed into and influence your ideas for each of the individual rooms you're going to decorate.

This moodboard (opposite), taken from a completed interiors scheme, represents the outcome of the research that went into it.

It clearly evokes a rich, dark and cosy space, balanced by pockets of contrasting light tones. Choosing colours that contain black pigment is a great way to achieve this, as it gives everything that lovely earthy shade. The inclusion of Lick's grounding Greige 02 with olive-toned Green 05, alongside visible-grain wooden samples, all complements this and enhances the natural feel.

Less literal elements – like the spool of ochre thread, brown paper envelope and dried wheat stems – all suggest gorgeous, faded autumn tones, and act as textural and colour references for the room's finishing touches.

Lick × SOHO HOUSE

Lick × SOHO HOUSE

GREIGE 02 SOHO WAREHOUSE

PEEL & STICK

Isla Finch

VELVET

NEPTUNE

Let's go on an image hunt

Alright, let's get started! Not only is this part of the process incredibly useful, it's also really fun. Remember, we're here to fire up our creativity and process ideas, not make any final decisions (yet); we're simply collecting images to help define your design direction.

Build on what we've already discussed by including ALL your references – from a pretty sunset snap on your camera roll to your favourite fashion accessory – along with more literal images of interiors and furniture (even if they're outlandish). Don't overthink it: if something about it appeals to you, include it, but if you're still unsure after five seconds, leave it out.

I suggest using Pinterest to pull it all together: you can set up a free account if you're not already on there. Create a board for your home or room and start 'pinning' images to it, whether they're your own photos or images you found online, or even from searching through Pinterest itself. As your board fills up, use the 'sections' feature to organise images by room (if your board represents your whole house), or break it down by categories like pattern, colour and furniture.

If you have any physical items you want to include in your scheme (such as images torn from a magazine or a physical object), either set them aside for the moment, or take photos of them and upload to your board so you're seeing the full picture in one place. Don't restrict yourself for now; just keep pinning and tune into the vibe and feeling you want to create. You'll soon see that 'red thread' emerging.

Tip

If you're tearing pages from magazines, choose a variety of titles and dates to avoid seeing only summer images, for example, or just one publication's particular aesthetic. Similarly, when saving pictures online, remember the algorithm feeds you what it thinks you like. While this is helpful to a degree, if you 'like' or pin lots of similar images it'll narrow down what it shows you, and you might find yourself in an echo chamber.

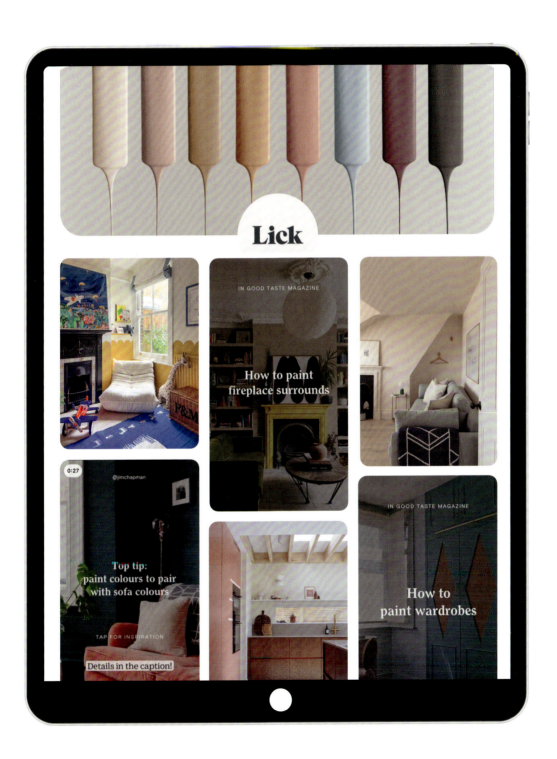

Create a shortlist of styles and samples

Once you're happy with your collection, step back and objectively analyse what you've got – are there any common themes emerging? Perhaps lots of your images contain a bright pop of yellow, or feature far more patterned sofas than plain ones?

Remember why you saved each image: was it one specific element you liked, or the overall atmosphere? Save these thoughts as notes against each image, and if there are any that you're not so keen on now, delete them (or create a 'maybe later' section).

Next, whittle them down and start grouping them into categories such as general mood, colour, pattern or furniture – whatever makes most sense to you. Have you ended up with lots of botanical patterns? Or picked mainly saturated tones when you initially thought you preferred light and bright spaces? Are many of the rooms filled with ornaments and houseplants, or are they pared back and minimal? Again, we're looking for those recurring red threads alongside any more literal inspo-shots.

Let's get physical

Now your ideas are clearer, you can start ordering and collecting all the samples of paints, wallpapers, fabrics, surfaces and materials you're planning to bring into your room. It's SO important to see these in the flesh (and in the room you'll use them in) as it's impossible to get a true sense of how everything will look and feel from a screen or photo. If you can, head to stores or showrooms stocking the materials or furniture you're considering to get a feel for them in situ.

If there are any major elements of your scheme you can't get physical swatches or samples for, or to represent any existing elements you're keeping, search for similar 'stand-in' samples so you can incorporate them into the mix to get the full picture. At this point you want to have a fairly focused idea of what you want and need, while still remaining open to flashes of unexpected inspiration.

Consider your...

+ **Colour palette:** does this broadly fit into a (maximum) three-key-hues framework (or five for a whole home)? This isn't about eliminating entire colour families, but checking you're using the best-suited tones and shades. Consider where – and in what ratios – you'd like to apply them.

+ **Desired mood and room orientation:** keeping these in mind allows you to instantly discount lots of individual colours and easily create a shortlist. For example, if you're after a dominant green for your small north-facing kitchen, you'll know you can skip the cooler tints.

+ **Existing elements:** don't overlook what's staying in the room (even if that includes elements you don't like but can't change – say, your landlord's choice of bright blue carpet). These need to be incorporated into your scheme either way. You might think this will highlight what you don't like, but, actually, repeating similar tones or materials elsewhere can help blend everything together and make those sore-thumb aspects less obvious.

Testing your samples at home

Now you've gathered all your samples, it's time to test them in the room you're decorating, so you're getting the full story. To kick off, lay them all down on the floor to get an overview: are there any that sit especially well together? Anything that feels a bit off? Hang on to them all for now, but make notes.

Testing your samples in situ:

Paint: stick your swatches to the surfaces you're thinking of painting that colour, such as walls, ceilings, woodwork, kitchen doors or a piece of furniture you're planning to repaint. At Lick, we offer 100% colour-accurate peel-and-stick swatches to make this bit really easy, but if you're also sampling colours from brands who sell tester pots instead, paint these onto a sheet of white paper (rather than directly onto your walls, which makes them immovable and can create shadow marks when painting over them). Cut out the white paper border once dry and write the brand and paint name on the back, then stick this to your relevant spot with some low-tack masking tape.

Wallpaper: use a decent-sized swatch (ideally at least A4-size), and stick it up in the area you're planning to use it with low-tack tape. For murals – or designs with a large pattern repeat – check your sample shows all the key colours and design elements, and source a picture of how it looks across a whole wall for reference.

Fabrics, flooring, tiles and other materials: place these in their intended spots. Lay upholstery swatches on your existing sofa, pin curtain samples to your current window treatment, place flooring samples on the floor… you get the picture. If its existing colour or pattern is throwing you off, cover it with a white sheet of fabric or paper first.

How to test

Leave the swatches in place for at least a day and observe them under the changing lighting conditions during both daylight hours and after dark, under artificial light. Then move them to other areas you'll be using them in, including contrasting spots like next to a window and in a darker corner. Note how the colours look when they receive more or less natural light. Make sure you also test against elements they'll be seen directly next to, like your sofa or wall art. Remember, it's generally easier to find paints to tie in with a multi-toned pattern, rather than finding patterns to match your paints.

Not sure what to choose? Honestly, go with your gut: deep down you WILL know what's right for you (and you'll be making an informed choice if you've read this far!). And remember that samples can potentially look starker or like more of a statement in isolation than they will in your finished scheme. Trust me – you can trust you! If you love it, it's the right choice.

A final scheme (and the sample tray that influenced it)

Before we move on to making your final moodboard, I want to share this stunning bathroom, created by the talented interior designer Emily Rickard, alongside the sample tray she created, which helped ensure the finished scheme matched the look and feel that both she and her client wanted to create.

Making a physical board or tray containing all your samples and swatches helps bring all of this to life and makes it more tangible and real (as well as helping you avoid any costly mistakes). It's also a lovely, tactile experience, which you don't get when you're working digitally. And it provides a proper sense of the scale of any patterns, both in relation to each other and to your room as a whole. Think of it as a working tool, rather than an end result, using it to tweak, reference and refine as you go.

The brief for this shower room (opposite) – designed for the homeowner's son – was for something fun and funky that had an evergreen design. To achieve this she opted for a pale neutral (White 06) on the walls, confining bolder green colour pops to the statement concrete sink and floor tiles, alongside splashes of dramatic black on the shower wall tiles and hardware accents.

The square of sheet metal indicated how her choice of brass plumbing and hardware fixtures would look within the overall mix, while the black hexagonal mosaics represent both the colour and crisp aesthetic style she wanted to bring into the finished space.

Create:
make a physical moodboard

In this Perfect Palette exercise, we'll apply everything we've learned so far to produce a fully-fledged moodboard. Bookmark this page so you can follow these steps for each scheme you create (or scan the QR code to access a downloadable version of this process).

Think of this like baking your favourite cake: we're checking off our ingredients and getting ready to combine everything to create something delicious.

You will need

Here's your visual ingredients list, based on the shortlist you've just worked on:

A board: a pinboard or even a tray works well for collating everything, and keeps things flexible. Go large if you can, so there's plenty of space to play.

Scissors (and tape, glue or sticky tack): for fixing anything down, if needed.

Your shortlisted swatches: include paints, wallpapers, upholstery or window fabrics, flooring, worktops and tiles, plus any 'placeholder' materials to represent fixed or large items already in the room.

A couple of 'hero' images: these should indicate the overall design direction, and can be literal – such as an image of an interior you love – as well as inspirational, like a photograph of a sunset that has inspired your colour palette. Print these out if they're digital files.

Smaller accents or hardware details: include a couple of smaller key items you plan to use in the space (like a door handle, curtain tieback or decorative light switch).

3D elements that bring in the vibe: conceptual pieces like a pretty seashell, small watercolour painting, handmade ceramic dish or a dried fern frond can help convey the overall mood. They can also help define the colours and textures of your scheme, or represent items you plan to include in the room (such as a collection of houseplants).

Optional: to get a 360-degree view, you could also include print-outs of key furniture and accessories you'll be using in the space, which you already own or are planning to buy.

How to combine the ingredients

1. Gather everything together and make sure you've got space to play. Pop down your board or tray, or just arrange everything directly on your tabletop then transfer it across when you're done.

2. Start with your hero images to set the tone, placing these in the middle of your surface. Next, bring in your paint swatches (unless the scheme is led by a patterned fabric or wallpaper). Start layering up your other elements around these, and see where it takes you.

3. Keep your proportions in mind and refer to the 60/30/10 ratio when it comes to your room palette. Lay down the paint swatches in roughly these proportions (page 189 has a template you can use). For wallpaper or textile samples, use larger samples to represent designs that will be dominant in the space, and fold or cut down swatches which represent accents, to give a clear sense of how they will work in the overall mix.

4. Once you're done, take a photo of the whole arrangement to refer back to when you're out and about (you can then remove any specific samples you want to take with you to shops or showrooms without worrying about messing your board up or having to take the whole thing). Keep an accompanying list of all your chosen paints, fabrics and materials, whether on a spreadsheet, in a notebook or stored on your phone: this makes it easier to share with tradespeople if needed, too.

Once you're happy, mentally sign this off. Congratulations! You've now locked in your palette and chosen your main elements. Remember, the goal isn't to make a pretty composition (even though I'm sure it will be), but to indicate how the finished space will look and feel, so you can feel confident in your design decisions, clear on what extra additions might work, and avoid any mid-decorating wobbles.

Design a digital reference board

Alongside your physical moodboard, you could also create a digital board to complement this (totally optional, but it can help when managing larger multi-room projects, or if you want a digital overview that pulls all your visual references into a single spot). This could focus more on the finalised elements you'll be using in your space, from accessories you plan to buy to existing items you might bring in.

It's up to you how you organise it, but the simple mock-up below shows the sorts of elements you might want to include. Canva is a great tool for creating these types of layouts, but there are lots of other apps which let you try moodboarding digitally, too (or you could even just add your images into a Google doc or PowerPoint slideshow).

Lay out your Lick samples by colour ratio proportions

While you don't have to be too exact when you're arranging paint swatches into a 60/30/10 ratio, sometimes it's helpful to have some guidelines. The page opposite features an outline you can directly lay your Lick swatches on top of to get the ratios spot on and give you a clearer idea.

My kitchen inspiration

Floor tile options

Layered lighting

Soften with plants

Hardware style

GREEN 06   WHITE 03

Potential paint colours

Free standing cabinet

Bar stools x3

Kitchen image @_beth_davis; product images from @blackbydesign2010, @cultfurniture, @dowsingandreynolds, @hyperiontilesltd, @indigenousltduk, @plankhardware, @scaramangau

1. Place your accent swatch here

2. Lay your sub-dominant swatch over it here

3. Then put your dominant swatch on the top here –
this will provide your 60/30/10 colour balance. Play
with the order to see what a difference it can make.
This will provide your ratios and you can then play
around with which might work best in each spot.

Amira's eclectic, travel-inspired home

Amira's one of my favourite clients and she's also a really good friend, so I loved having the opportunity to help her curate this colour palette. When she viewed the property, she could see its potential and, despite being a first-time buyer, wasn't afraid to take on structural work so she could put her own stamp on the place and create her perfect layout. Although her style is mixed and eclectic, she takes quite a rigorous approach to home design, using her editor's eye to hone in on an object or place she feels inspired by. From there, she'll search through her archive of materials samples collected over the years and play around until she has created a look she wants to bring to life.

Mediterranean aesthetics – and those beautiful warm azures and teals that reflect them – were a big draw for her, so we pulled together a gorgeous paint palette which reflected this, adding in some grounding earthy colours alongside those sea-inspired tones. What she's so clever at doing is using design references in both subtle and overt ways, which creates this lovely authentic, layered look that's very personal to her. This then serves as a backdrop for her various trinkets and treasures (and the odd dash of her beloved kitschy bling).

Downstairs, Amira totally transformed the flow and feel of the space, turning several small, disjointed rooms into one generous living area and switching the positions of the kitchen and dining area to make better use of the space. Her new kitchen now sits in the middle of the house, allowing her now-dining spot to live at the back of the house, meaning guests can easily spill out into her courtyard garden when she's entertaining. To enhance this connection, she installed two sets of double doors (finished in a gorgeous vibrant green similar to Lick's Green 14) which helps draw the eye outside.

WHO LIVES HERE?

Amira Hashish, founder and editorial director of creative and publishing studio Rapport and lifestyle magazine *Neighbourhood Edit*.

INSTAGRAM

@thedesigneditor

THE PROPERTY

An old sweet shop previously converted into a home. The knocked-through, open-plan ground floor contains a living room at the front, kitchen in the middle and dining/ social space at the back leading directly out to a small garden. On the first floor is a home office, main bathroom, and a guest bedroom with en suite. In the converted loft space on the floor above is Amira's bedroom area, en suite and storage area.

PREFERRED COLOURS AND STYLES

Eclectic treasure trove with Mediterranean influences. Lots of trinkets and patterns play together but sit within a relatively restrained overall palette of blues, greens and the odd colour pop and splash of bling.

191

Rather than keep the white used by the previous owners, Amira opted to embrace her small living room by making it into more of a cosy snug. By wrapping the walls in Teal 01 – a beautiful, warm mid tone – she created a cocooning and cosy feel which lets the red and mustard tones in her furniture and accessories really pop.

The kitchen's new central position means it doesn't receive any direct sunlight (a common issue in long, skinny layouts). I suggested using light yet warm Taupe 03 here, to help balance this out: with its gentle red and grey undertones, it has a real nurturing feel (perfect for a kitchen) and sits beautifully against the tones in her marble worktop, and opposite the deliberately bare raw plaster walls of the dining room.

Amira's knack for blending different looks and styles is evident in her first floor bathroom and separate en suite: while the bathroom features traditional Victorian colours and patterns, including a statement brown floral patterned sink (which pairs beautifully with the Blue 13 walls and deep blue wall tiles), her en suite takes its style lead from the radically different aesthetic of traditional Moroccan baths. But with their shared brown tones and gold accents, they still retain a sense of flow. And she always finds THE most amazing pieces to finish her spaces with, thanks to her little black book of vintage dealers and reclamation yards (alongside scouring online marketplaces). These canny finds and vintage treasures allow her to add character while shopping sustainably.

On the top floor is Amira's own bedroom suite, which she designed from scratch after converting the loft to create an additional floor. Her bedroom repeats the same Taupe 03 used in the kitchen, bringing that red thread repetition to the top of the house, where its tone actually looks very different in this light-flooded space. Featuring an en suite and a floor-to-ceiling window at one end, she's added a cute bistro table in this corner to create a holiday-suite-at-home feel (all that's missing is those views of the Med).

Amira's core house palette

KEY PARENT COLOURS

LEADING LICK PAINT PICKS

BEIGE 03

TAUPE 03

GREEN 09

BLUE 13

TEAL 01

'I really relished the challenge of turning this previously bland home into a space that perfectly suits my needs - it's such a fun retreat and a place I love spending time in. I love blending different eras, materials and colours to create design schemes that tell a story.

I knew I wanted to showcase the building's Victorian heritage while also bringing in sunny Mediterranean influences. Working with Tash enabled me to find the right palette to hold it all together and help my various design elements sit harmoniously in the space, which really helped my confidence during the process of creating this. As soon as people step into my home, I hope they feel the same sense of warmth and joy that it brings me.'

– AMIRA –

Pulling it all together

This final chapter is almost like a tale of two halves, bringing together everything we've learned so far and sharing the practical final steps needed to execute and complete your scheme.

First we'll focus on my takeaway tips for choosing and combining all of your furniture, accessories, ornaments, hardware and art. While this is a big topic, I've broken it down into some key 'golden rules' that you can apply to get you up and running.

And, of course, it would be remiss for any decorating book – especially one written by the interiors director of a paint brand – not to tell you exactly HOW to best approach painting in terms of the prep and practical steps, so I'll also demystify that side of things, so you're primed to bring your scheme to life.

6

My golden styling rules

Choosing and arranging your furnishings, accessories and decorative touches can be the key to pulling your space together and giving it a curated feel. We'll discuss individual examples in the coming pages, but there are also some general rules to follow here, which broadly apply to everything from clever furniture placements to stylish shelf arrangements (aka a 'shelfie').

Playing with shapes

The way individual elements and their collective shapes (or smaller arrangements of objects) come together can dramatically transform the ambiance of a whole room.

Create structure: arrange furniture, accessories and art so that they relate to each other. This could mean visually anchoring them with another element (a large rug underneath a dining table and chairs, or housing several smaller ornaments on a tray, for example), or arranging them strategically (such as hanging a collection of differently sized artworks so that the overall outline forms a rectangular shape).

Create flow and movement: purposefully mix different heights and shapes to guide the eye around the space (or across a smaller arrangement). Play with different shape combinations as well, to enhance this flow (such as breaking up blocky furniture with curves or rounded corners).

Filling the space

How you arrange your furniture and objects – and how much space you leave purposefully empty – can help to create harmony. The same general rules apply from the macro (furniture) to the micro (trinkets on a tray).

Pair similar proportions: choose pieces that fit well together (whether that's within their intended spot or in proportion to one another) without any jarring extremes of size. Group smaller pieces strategically in curated clusters, or use furniture sets to define areas for different activities.

Balance negative space: judiciously use spots of 'nothing' between your arrangements to ensure things don't feel cramped. These offer respite for the eye, but make sure they're well-proportioned so you don't accidentally create oddly large or weirdly small gaps in awkward spots.

Layering different styles

Creating a cohesive and authentic style requires blending different (and sometimes opposing) elements together to create repetition.

Watch for the red thread: find the common factors that tie your room (and home) together, such as repeated colours, design motifs, shapes and materials. How are you using these?

Opposites attract: add in an element of juxtaposition so the space feels lived-in and personal. Bring something vintage into a contemporary room scheme, add some tactility to a room filled with hard surfaces, mix shiny textures with matt or pair bold, graphic patterns with smaller, delicate prints. The same applies to functional areas too, such as breaking up a bookshelf with a few ornaments or pieces of art.

Furniture

Aside from accent pieces like a side table or slim shelving unit, furniture often takes up a huge chunk of your floor space, especially in a smaller home. This means it's naturally going to form a dominant part of your room, so make sure it's something you're happy to draw attention to. If it's something you're not keen on but can't switch out, you might want to strategically choose a similar-coloured backdrop so it blends in somewhat.

Four furniture layout floorplans

I've created these floorplans of a living room and bedroom to show the impact that furniture placement can have on a space. Both are based on the same size room and key furniture items, but this bird's-eye view demonstrates how easy it can be to inadvertently create a cluttered look.

One living room, two ways

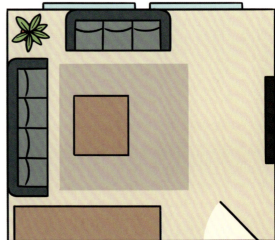

AWESOME

+ Front legs of the sofa sit on the rug, making it feel generous in size.

+ A single L-shaped sofa pulled away from the walls creates a zoned seating nook.

+ Oval coffee table breaks up the rectangles of the sofa and rug, and is comfortable to navigate around.

+ Console unit on the back wall provides out-of-sight storage, and fills a redundant gap which might otherwise look empty.

AWKWARD

+ Two individual sofas lined along the walls feels disjointed – and a little like you're walking into a waiting room.

+ Square coffee table means you're entering the room facing a sharp corner, which can feel uninviting (as can lots of straight edges with few curves to balance them out).

+ Console unit fills up a third wall and is more visibly dominant, creating a cluttered feel.

Ono bedroom, two ways

AWESOME

+ Bed placement feels comfortable in the room, there's a direct view of the window.

+ Circular bedside tables balance the large rectangular shape of the bed.

+ One large rug defines the whole sleeping area.

+ Wardrobe feels unobtrusive.

+ Ottoman offers storage at the end of the bed, and can double up as a window seat.

+ Chair in the corner provides a cosy reading spot.

AWKWARD

+ Bed placement feels uncomfortable: the door-side sleeper could feel exposed.

+ Square bedside tables mean walking directly in to a blocky piece of furniture.

+ Two skinny rugs creates more visual clutter and makes the floorspace look smaller.

+ View from the bed is of the wardrobe rather than the window.

+ No space for the ottoman at the foot of the bed – this position makes it more of an obstacle.

+ Chair in the corner feels cramped.

Accents and accessories

Often referred to as the 'finishing touches', the smaller accents and accessories we bring into our rooms actually make a massive impact on how well a space looks, feels and visually hangs together. They can reinforce our overall scheme through repeating key motifs, colours and materials; just like adding seasoning to our food, they bring a sprinkle of spice that takes things up several notches.

What should I choose?

+ Items you love! Please remember this first and foremost over buying things that match your 10% accent colour but you don't feel a connection to. Bring in keepsakes from favourite places you've visited, family heirlooms or objects that express your personality, tastes or cultural heritage.

+ Plan in a few opposites-attract pieces, such as something handmade or vintage to break up a mainly modern space. Designers often advise bringing a touch of black into every room as it can add contrast and depth, helping to anchor the room. Metallic accents and reflective surfaces can also help lift the space and bounce light around.

+ Houseplants not only look great, but they also bring nature into the home and can positively impact our mental health. You could choose your plant babies to tie in with the general vibe of your space; for example, bring cacti into a warm, tropical-style scheme, monstera and spider plants for a retro look, or ferns in a Victorian home. There are plenty of other natural treasures you could bring in too, such as sculptural branches or a textural bit of bark found on a country walk.

How to curate a styling arrangement

While these arrangements can give you a great styling steer, try not to get too caught up on the specifics: it's YOUR home, not a show home, so if you love your four-vase arrangement, it should stay (but you could see how it looks if you throw in a smaller fifth item, too).

Create structure: just as rugs can help zone a floor space, so too can trays (or even coffee table books, laid horizontally) help to zone sideboards and tabletops. Again, mixing in accessories with different heights, sizes and shapes on these surface tops creates visual interest.

If you DO want to create a symmetrical arrangement, make sure it's bang on: this can work really well on a console table (like the example opposite) if you use a pair of identical lamps at either end then add a single statement item in the middle, like a plant or floral display. Add in a few non-matching grouped items in the gaps to soften the formality.

Create flow and movement: our eyes tend to favour odd numbers, so objects arranged as two groups of three and two – rather than four or six individual objects spread across your shelf or surface – looks chic and a lot more curated.

The illustration opposite shows how playing with their heights and shapes also gives the eye something to move around, while keeping things overlapping helps reinforce these as 'groups' rather than disparate items.

1

@buildbysets; walls in Greige 02

2

Art

Art effortlessly brings a room to life and make it feel finished (without any art on the walls, a room will always seem lacking). I adore art – so much so, I originally trained as a fine artist – and I've always hung my favourite works in every place I've called home. In fact, my art usually forms the foundation of my personal decorating schemes.

How to choose art

I've picked out some colour ideas (shown in the swatches below) which pull out lighter tints and darker tones from this artwork without directly copying it. For this sitting area, we chose a colour scheme that proportionally reflects the dominant off-whites, sub-dominant pinks and 10% black accents of the art, but if these ratios were reversed it would look equally amazing.

+ Consider what story the art is telling and why you love it; is it the style, subject matter or a memory it evokes (like a painting picked up on your honeymoon, or a city skyline you adore)?

+ Creatively integrate art into your décor, finding a unifying palette or style (rather than necessarily an exact 'match'). The same applies to multiple artworks that share a wall or space.

+ Art doesn't have to be 'art' – get creative with what you hang on your walls! A vintage plate, hand-stitched tapestry or cute postcard can add personality and help break up a bunch of rectangular frames, while strategically filling any awkward gaps.

@buildbysets; walls in Pink 02, Gucci wallpaper in frames
Photo: @emmalewisphotographer

...and how to arrange it

To ensure a feature wall looks impactful rather than messy, choose one guiding principle to follow (which will simplify rather than limit the process).

If you're unsure where to start, lay everything out on your floor first so you can visualise and tweak the composition. Resist the urge to hang everything with huge gaps in between to fill your whole wall: it'll look far more impactful if you keep the arrangement tight.

TRY THESE THREE APPROACHES:

1. Align your edges: use the edges of your outer frames to create a square or rectangular shape. This will result in uneven spaces between pieces, but the overall structure will tie it all together.

2. Even spacing: try the opposite, keeping gaps between each piece (relatively) even. The overall outline won't be a uniform shape, but will give a casual feel that's easier to expand outwards as your collection grows.

3. Go for a grid: arrange same-sized frames into a neat grid, with even spaces between them all for a sleek, graphic look. This does, however, require fairly meticulous hanging as the slightest deviation will be more noticeable.

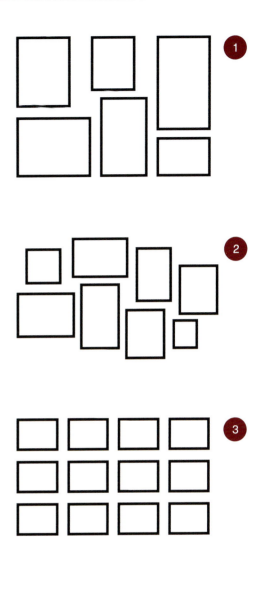

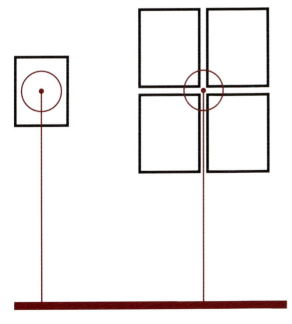

Tip

Avoid hanging your art too high: take your lead from the experts (aka art galleries), who typically hang works so that the centre of each piece (or the central piece in a feature wall) is around 145cm (50 in) from the floor, aligning roughly with the average eye line.

Fixtures and fittings

Fixtures and fittings play a small but mighty part in your overall design scheme, holding the power to transform a room from meh to wow! Some, like light fittings, electrical switches, taps and radiators need factoring in early during renovations, while others, such as door handles, hooks and drawer pulls, can be added any time. Often referred to as the 'jewellery of the home', there are so many stunning options out there, from beautiful gemstone door handles to a statement hardware back plates.

Hide or highlight?

Highlighting fixtures and fittings with contrasting, statement designs or colours is a great way to enhance your scheme: think of a stunning floor-standing bath tap, or a charming vintage-inspired cast-iron radiator.

Hide less-lovely fixtures by painting them the same colour as the walls they're in front of, or by choosing 'invisible' fittings like switches and socket plates. And if your radiators are basic white models, ALWAYS paint them the same colour as your walls when repainting a room, otherwise they'll stand out like a sore thumb. This simple step is often overlooked, but it makes SUCH a difference (Lick's paints are suitable for metals, so you can use your wall paint here, too).

Choosing metals

Warm metals have become really popular in interiors over the past decade (though there's a lot of love for cooler chromes, too). Traditionally, it's recommended to use just one metal per room, within a similar-toned palette (such as warm gold or brass in a pink and brown scheme, or cool steel with blues and greys). This approach works – and is a great option for more harmonious schemes – but using opposite-toned metals can look really striking, too.

Mixed-metal schemes can also look stunning, although I'd limit it to two per room, using the same metal across plumbing fixtures then bringing in a second metal for handles, light fittings or hooks. For an eclectic feel, mix matching metals with different design styles or finishes, such as a shiny tap spout with textural hammered handles.

Different types and tones of metals

Warm

Gold

Rose gold

Antique gold

Copper

Brass

Antique brass

Bronze

Antique bronze

Cool

Chrome

Stainless steel

Neutral

Cast iron

Black metal

Renter-friendly decorating ideas

So many of us now rent now into our 30s and beyond (myself included!), and even those who have climbed onto the property ladder often have to wait a while before they can afford the renovations they've set their heart on. But I'm a big believer in making the most of what you've got (even if it's not 'yours') – so whatever your limitations, there are always ways we can improve our surroundings (and in turn, our happiness). Here's a few key areas to consider:

Workarounds for using paint and wallpaper

Paint is such an easy (and inexpensive) way to create a major impact. If your landlord permits painting but wants the walls returned to white at the end of your tenancy, see if they'd compromise and let you repaint (and leave in place) warm, neutral colours instead. Otherwise, contain your colours to key rooms and areas so there's less to paint back when you move. Alternatively, add paint or wallpaper to your own furniture instead.

Give a glow-up with textiles

If your rental includes your landlord's taste in window treatments and furniture, consider ways you can hide them to create a space that's more to your taste.

Replace existing curtains with your own, storing the originals safely (IKEA is a great place to source inexpensive curtains and material, or search designer fabric discount outlets for a bargain). Cover an ugly sofa with several strategically placed and neatly tucked throws (rather than a giant dust sheet-style one), and hide any existing cushions in plain sight by adding your own covers to them.

Add art without messing up your walls

Choosing lightweight artwork options like canvas paintings or Perspex (rather than glass) frames lets you skip the hooks and nails and use removable picture-hanging strips instead. Alternatively, ask your landlord if you can fix up a picture ledge (a shallow shelf with a lip at the front, which can be fixed to walls with a couple of screws), to minimise wall damage and provide a spot to casually display a collection of art (or cool book covers and favourite LP sleeves). Or simply place larger or heavier pieces on cabinet tops and let them lean against the wall for a laid-back, fixing-free look.

Superficially revamp your kitchen

Switching out basic cupboard handles can be transformative (simply pop your landlord's back in and take yours with you when you move on). There's also a wealth of decorative stickers for tiles (and vinyl sheets for cupboard doors) which can give an impactful transformation and should come off without causing any damage (though do test in an inconspicuous area first). You could even remove and store the doors from wall units to create an open shelving look, offering you extra styling space to add your own personality.

Even if you own your home, you may not have the budget for a full-on kitchen replacement. Alanna opted to transform the bare bones of her inherited rundown kitchen without making costly changes – and she absolutely nailed this assignment. Her existing chipboard worktops became the base for beautiful pink metro tiles, which continue part-way up the walls as a splashback. Removing the shabby doors from her base units and replacing them with a cabinet skirt brings softness (a trick she also used to hide an ugly fire door).

Existing wall units were switched out for inexpensive open shelves, which Alanna personalised with MDF scallop trim, a splash of statement yellow paint and a hanging rail to store and display her pretty kitchenware. The walls and ceiling – finished in Lick's Pink 13 – bring the room together to create a super-cosy feel.

Before you start

Alright, we're ready to bring everything to life! But before you pick up that brush, let's run through some of the basics you'll need to know, so the whole process goes swimmingly.

Paint types and finishes

Paint used to be pretty toxic, filled with harmful materials and requiring noxious white spirit to clean up afterwards. Fortunately, things are far cleaner and greener these days, with water-based paints now considered the norm. All Lick's paints are water-based, and contain just a trace amount of VOCs, meaning fewer chemicals and better air quality in the home. Our paint tins and packaging are all recyclable, too.

Thanks to improvements in paint technology, it's also easier to choose your paint finish based on personal style preference, rather than dictated by practical requirements. Traditionally, higher-sheen paints like satin and gloss were required for durability on high traffic areas or tricky surfaces, as well as in areas that needed to be easily wipeable. This usually meant buying several paints in various sheens to cater for the different surface types in a single room, whether you wanted a mixed look or not.

One of the things I'm proudest of at Lick is our innovative formulas, which mean you can choose any of our colours in either a matt (low sheen) or eggshell (soft sheen) finish, and they all work wonderfully on pretty much any surface (the odd instances when you do need to use an additional primer are flagged later in this chapter). This makes life so much easier and also allows you to easily colour drench different surfaces, all from the same tin. If you DO want a glossy look, you can add a high-sheen decorator's varnish on top, but it gives the choice back to you.

How to prep

What you need will depend on your surface (and the condition it's in), but here are the main supplies you'll need and steps to follow for most prep work:

PREPPING TOOLS

A basic cleaning kit: you'll want a bucket of warm, soapy water, a large sponge, rubber gloves and a clean, dry duster.

A step ladder: tall enough to comfortably reach your ceilings or the top of your walls.

Stripping knife: for scraping and removing any blemishes, previous paint or surface finishes.

Filler and filling knife: for filling superficial holes and cracks.

Protective sheets to cover flooring and furniture.

Sandpaper or a sanding sponge: a fine grit will suffice for most surfaces, unless you're painting a fairly rough wooden surface.

STEPS

Clear some space: pull furniture away from surfaces or trims you'll be painting (or if what you're painting IS your furniture, make sure you can easily access all the areas you'll need to prep and paint). Lay down protective sheeting anywhere that might receive dust and paint splatters.

Complete an initial surface clean with some warm soapy water, then rinse. This will ensure any fillers will bind properly to your surface. Inspect surfaces as you go, noting any areas of damage such as holes, cracks, flaky plaster or peeling paint. Allow to dry.

Repair your surfaces: use a filler appropriate for your surface type to remedy those damaged spots, working it into holes or cracks with your filler knife, then smooth it off and let dry. For any particularly flaky bits, a stripping knife could come in handy. If you're prepping wood that's covered in thick layers of paint, strip it off with a heat gun for the best finish.

Sand your entire surface with sandpaper or a sanding sponge to ensure a smooth surface for your paint to adhere. For walls, use a circular motion (and don't go too heavy). For wooden surfaces, follow the grain of the wood: keep things light if it's an untreated surface; if it's been previously painted and varnished, start with a medium-grit sandpaper to remove any surface sheen.

Do a final clean-up: dust your surface down with a dry cloth, then give it a final soapy water clean and rinse (clean surrounding floors and surfaces, too). Once it's dry, you're ready to move on to painting. Certain surfaces, like composite or solid woods as well as uPVC, may need priming – check on page 218 if you're not sure.

Order of works

Now you've completed all your prep, it's time to crack open the paint tins and let the magic commence! Here are the tools you'll need and steps to follow so you can paint like a pro.

Painting tools

Your paint! If you've not ordered this yet, Lick's website has a paint calculator to help you work out how much you'll need.

Paintbrushes: it's handy to have a few flat brushes of different widths for smaller spots and larger areas. Angled brushes are useful for 'cutting in' (the technique used to paint a neat, precise edge at the point where two different colours or surfaces meet). A longer artist's paint brush can also be handy for awkward nooks and crevices when painting radiators or furniture.

Paint roller and tray: a 23cm (9 in) frame with a mid-pile sleeve works well for most surfaces, or try a 10cm (4 in) frame with a short-pile sleeve for smaller cabinetry and furniture, for a texture-free finish. A roller extension pole can be handy for high ceilings.

Protective gear: it's wise to wear safety glasses and a mask when painting (as well as your least-favourite outfit). Use protective sheets on floors and surfaces, as before.

Masking tape: a good low-tack painter's tape will help you keep within the lines (for best results, always remove it gently before the paint is dry, and use fresh tape for second coats).

Before you start, prep your paint by stirring it thoroughly in its tin to ensure it's well blended (all Lick paints are sent with a stirring stick). If your project requires several tins of the same colour, it's a good idea to 'box' the paint first (pour every tin into one large container, then mix thoroughly): this will ensure that any slight variations between the tins will be evenly mixed across each batch. Most surfaces will require two coats, so factor this into your overall painting time.

Try this:

+ Allow 2–4 hours for each coat to dry (and ideally 24 hours before placing furniture back against freshly painted walls). For painted furniture and cabinetry, it can take a week or so for the paint to fully 'cure' (even when it's dry to the touch, paints take longer to reach maximum hardness and durability), so try to avoid placing items on their tops – or using cleaning sprays on their surface – during this time.

+ Avoid overloading your brush when painting – aim to cover the bristles half-way. Try placing an elastic band across the centre of your tin, to wipe away any excess when you're loading up and prevent the edge of your paint tin getting crusted up.

+ To save washing your brushes and rollers out during drying times, wrap them in – ideally biodegradable – cling film (plastic wrap) to stop the paint drying out.

+ Use a sheet of paper or card instead of masking tape when painting edges where there's a join or slight gap, such as where your skirting board meets the floor, or between window frames and glazing.

STEPS

If you're painting a whole room, start at the top and work your way down. Here's how to handle each area:

Ceilings: apply masking tape around the tops of your walls (unless you're drenching the same colour across ceilings and walls) and over the base of light fittings. Using a brush (2.5cm/1 in angled is ideal), start to 'cut in' from the perimeter of the ceiling by around 7–10cm (3–4 in), then switch to your roller to fill in a broader section. Continue working your way around the edges and into the centre of the ceiling in small sections, always rolling in the same direction to reduce visible roller tracks showing when dry. If you're drenching, lap the paint onto the tops of walls for a neater finish when you come to paint these.

Cornicing: if you're painting this in a separate colour to both your walls and ceilings, mask these both off before painting around the room with a brush (the same technique applies if you're adding a contrasting coloured band of paint in the same area). Otherwise, incorporate with your wall or ceiling treatments, as appropriate.

Walls: apply masking tape around the edges of adjoining woodwork (such as skirting boards, window frames and door frames). Using your angled brush, repeat the same process used on your ceiling, cutting in at the corner of one wall then using your roller to fill in the main area, working methodically across each wall in sections. Move your roller in 'W' or 'M' motions for even distribution.

Woodwork: mask off walls and floors, then use your angled brush for the edges, switching to a flat brush for the main surfaces, if you prefer.

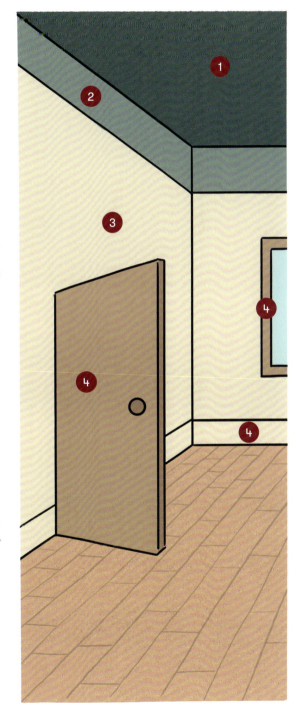

Make simple patterns with paint

Now you know the basics, you can progress to creating simple shapes and patterns on your walls (and hopefully have a little fun, too). I've shared two easy techniques to create both stripes and circular (or arched) shapes with ease, which you can adapt for your dream design: this doesn't require any artistic skill, just a little prep and planning, yet it gives really impressive results. Whether you want to create single shapes or create a more elaborate design, these techniques can form the starting point to spark your own ideas. As well as your freshly painted walls, you'll need brushes, protective gear and paint; and grab a tape measure, spirit level and a pencil. To create curves, you'll also need a length of string, a thin nail or push pin, and a hammer.

Painted bands and rectangles

Using masking tape as a mid-wall barrier allows you to create lines, stripes and shapes, from dividing a wall horizontally with a 50/50 design (using two different colours on its upper and lower halves) to more decorative patterns like a chequerboard design or statement diagonal stripes.

STEPS

Use your tape measure, pencil and spirit level to measure out and mark where you want your painted line(s) to sit. Stick your masking tape down against these pencil lines to section off the area you'll be adding your accent colour to, or to divide your wall in half.

Paint over the edges of the masking tape in the area you'll be applying your accent area, but use the same paint colour that's already on the wall. This will fill any tiny gaps and create a seal, preventing your accent colour from bleeding through once it's added. Leave the tape in place and let dry.

Use a brush or roller to paint your accent colour in this area, going slightly over the sealed tape edges, then remove the masking tape while it's still wet. Let dry, then repeat the process if a second coat is required.

Pattern with curves

Curved shapes look welcoming and bring a softness to any room. They can create a statement area, such as a semicircular painted 'headboard', or for subtler touches like smaller overlapping circles. Here are two key techniques to try:

Use a template: take a curved or circular shape (like a plate) and draw around it directly onto your wall. If you're creating a repeat pattern – such as painting a half-scallop edge along a wall – you might find it easier to trace your shape onto a piece of card, creating a lightweight, flat template you can tape to the wall as you work.

Create a string guideline: decide on the overall size and shape you want for your curve and where its centre should be, then pop a small nail or push pin into your wall at that spot. Take a length of string and tie one end to the pin, attaching a pencil to the other end. Pull it taut to guide you as you draw on your curved line.

For both methods, once you've created your shape, fill it in with your accent paint using a steady hand and a good brush.

After

Trix really has worked wonders with this kitchen makeover: as a renter, she made the most of what was already there by, with her landlord's permission, repainting the existing kitchen unit doors in Green 05, as well as upgrading their handles, which really lifted the space. But there's no denying it's this chequerboard feature wall that brings it all to life and gives it so much personality.

Create a checkerboard

Mark out your square shapes on your wall with a pencil and long ruler. Stick your masking tape down inside the pencil lines of every other square, using a sharp craft knife to cut the tape neatly in the corners, so they're crisp.

Your squares without tape inside their boundaries are the ones you'll be painting in a contrasting colour, but initially, paint over their inside edges with your main wall colour, as per step two of painted bands, to prevent bleeding. Once dry, add two coats of your contrasting colour, using a short roller. Remove the masking tape, then touch up if needed.

Tip: If you're a visual learner, search through Trix's Instagram to see her own tutorial for this project.

Before

Upcycle your furniture

There's far more you can paint than just walls - and painting furniture is often a more affordable approach and environmentally responsible option, too (compared to buying something new). It's also a brilliant way to use up any leftovers of paint (for smaller jobs, at least). Winning!

In the context of interiors, upcycling usually means elevating an existing item in some way, whether to enhance its appearance (such as painting a tired piece of furniture or making a new cover for an old armchair), or to improve its functionality (like adding wheel castors to a coffee table's legs so you can easily move it around the room, or repurposing a stool that has a broken seat into a plant pot stand).

How to paint freestanding furniture

Just as with walls, mask off any areas like handles (or sections you don't want to paint) with masking tape. Start applying your paint at the edges then work your way down, either using a small roller, a brush, or a bit of both, keeping your strokes consistent. If your piece has any protruding mouldings, paint these first.

Here are a few simple styles to try:

+ Break up a blocky piece with a variety of colours: use a different colour on every drawer, or paint the top third of a cabinet in a contrasting colour to the rest (this can bring a fun modern twist to older furniture).

+ Try a part-painted approach, leaving elements of natural wood exposed, for example painting your tabletop but leaving its legs untouched.

+ Use masking tape to create simple patterns and shapes, adapting the wall mural advice from the previous page.

Upcycling furniture with paint

From simple colour changes to elaborate patterns, the only limit is your imagination. While painting older wooden furniture is a fairly common choice, paint is a brilliant way to elevate modern flat-pack pieces, too.

Here's how to prime most furniture surfaces (following the earlier steps on pages 212–213):

Surface type one: composite wood (such as laminate, melamine or veneer), which is an engineered surface wrapped around a particleboard.

How to spot: these might look like a natural material, but look closer. Is the pattern smooth, neat and uniform? Does it have a plastic-look sheen? Is it relatively lightweight, or does it sound hollow when you tap it? If so, it's probably not the real deal (the same applies for plain-coloured surfaces, which will likely look too 'perfect' to be a hand-painted surface).

How to prime: lightly sand the surface using a fine grit sandpaper, clean, then apply a coat of hardwearing primer suitable for this surface type (I'd recommend Zinsser B-I-N® Aqua water-based primer or LickPro interior primer and undercoat). Let dry, then add your final paint.

Surface type two: solid wood or MDF.

How to spot: untreated solid wood will have a matt appearance and subtle irregularities in its grain. Engineered wood (MDF) has a uniform flat brown finish.

How to prime: these surfaces can be quite absorbent and porous so create a 'mist coat' to prime them with (a mix of 70% of your chosen paint and 30% water); this will help your final undiluted paint to adhere. If the wood has been previously painted and is in good condition, you can go straight from prepping to painting (otherwise, refer back to page 213 for best prep steps).

@nicolejanelle; cupboard in Green 05

Good to know

While all Lick paints can be used on any of these primed surface types, that's not necessarily the case for all brands. If you're planning to use a paint from elsewhere, always check the tin to make sure it's suitable.

@houseonthecorner_16; drawers in Red 01

Elevate your fitted units

Built-in cabinets and storage – such as kitchen units, bathroom vanities and fitted wardrobes – are perfect candidates to transform with a little paint, too. If your existing doors or units are fundamentally sound and their layout works, it makes much more sense to paint rather than replace them.

Check if the materials are solid or composite wood, then prep, prime and paint accordingly. Where possible, remove cupboard doors but leave their hinges intact, making them easier to paint and rehang, then remove any handles (or protect them with masking tape) before painting.

Stand out or blend in?

For random cupboards in odd spots, I'd suggest painting them the same colour as surrounding walls, to help them 'disappear'. But for kitchen doors or an island unit, have fun with adding a little colour; consider a darker tone and lighter tint of the same colour for base and wall units.

For fitted wardrobes (which are something I'm asked about a lot) the choice really depends on both your space and mood goals. If your fitted wardrobes are a little obtrusive, go for the same (or a tonally similar) colour as your walls, but if it's quite a pretty piece – and your room doesn't have any other focal points – go ahead and paint it a contrasting colour instead, to form part of your 30% sub-dominant palette.

@elizabethstanhope; cabinets in Blue 04 and White 03

@laura.elizabeth_ ; fitted wardrobes in Grey 07

Transform your window frames

Unless you're lucky enough to have beautiful wooden window frames (or a cool Crittall style, made from slim steel), chances are you've probably got white uPVC designs in your home. And while these are a smart and hardwearing option, the bright white finish can sometimes look a little jarring, especially in rooms decorated in darker tones.

If you'd like to blend yours in – or perhaps even draw attention to a view by painting them in a contrasting tone – follow the same prep-steps as for composite wood on page 218, then finish with any Lick paint (or other paint suitable for this surface type). It's generally best to hold off painting recently installed units for at least a year, as they tend to come with a coating that's difficult to paint over.

You can use the same approach for a uPVC porch or conservatory, and it can be utterly transformative – as these before and after photos show – can you even believe this is the same room?!

After

Before

@lets.stay.at.home; woodwork in Green 05

221

Summarise:
crack your own colour code

This last exercise isn't really an exercise at all, it's a place where you can finalise everything you've learned about your decorating self so far, and where you can plan out all your future projects. Because now you know what you want and need, you'll be able to streamline all your design decision-making and avoid any angst.

As always, you can answer these questions in a notebook, or download a PDF sheet to fill in from the website link in this QR code. And while you're there, check out all the other bonus links and resources I've been sharing for my readers, too!

My colour personality

Think of this as a steer for all your decorating endeavours – almost like an 'ultimate source of truth' that is by you, about you. Often our answers don't fit neatly into one option, or our thoughts are dependent on circumstance, so include notes alongside these to provide context.

My preferences for	Are (choose your own based on the prompts below)
 Colour temperature	Cool, warm, balanced, a mix of temperatures
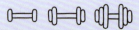 Colour weight	Light, mid, balanced, a mix of weights, don't have a strong preference
 Colour relationships	Low contrast (monochromatic), harmonious contrast (analogous and dyadic), a stronger contrast (complementary), a broader palette to play with (triadic/split complementary/tetradic)
 Colour balances	I prefer my 60/30/10 balance of colours to be a neutral dominant colour, bolder sub-dominant colour and a dark accent colour
 Interior moods	Light & airy (pale, neutral tones; cooler colours) Calm & relaxing (balanced, darker neutrals; nature connection) Cosy & warm (rich, earthy tones; a comforting feel) Dark & moody (deep, lush colours; cocooning atmosphere) Energising (saturated, lively colours; mixed weights and intensities)

My project

We've talked lots about the choices you might make in certain rooms – here's the space to write down the specifics of what they'll be, to create a room renovation crib sheet. You don't need to fill this in until you're actively planning or undertaking a project, but keep this ready with your other Perfect Palette exercises for when you do.

Take a final moment before wrapping this up to check your colour personality responses tally with your room project choices: did you put down that you're a light and airy type, but your room plans contain lots of saturation and contrast? The final check-in that you always need to do is ultimately with your gut.

My design brief	Key info, plans and details
The room I'm decorating is...	e.g. my bedroom
Its orientation is...	north, south, east, west, dual aspect
The key hues of my overall scheme are...	which 1–3 parent colours are you using as the basis for your palette? For example, blue, green and orange – see chapter 5 if you need to refresh your memory
The specific paint colours I'm going to use within this palette are...	list these out, along with their colour balances and where you plan to use them; for example, I'm going to use Green 14 as my dominant colour on my walls and ceiling, then... and so on
I want to use paint strategically to...	e.g. make my short room look taller, hide an ugly radiator, highlight my fireplace
I'm going to bring in pattern through...	e.g. wallpaper, upholstery, tiles, key accessories – write down specific patterns and colourways
My key furniture pieces (and their role in creating my palette) are going to be...	e.g. my sofa is teal and is part of my sub-dominant blue palette
I'll layer in character with...	e.g. my granny's vintage armchair, my handmade Moroccan wedding blanket

INSIDE SCOOP:
WHY GINA POWELL
IS A T-SHIRT
LIFTER!

WHO ARE THE
LIPPER-LICKERS?
AND THE
IT-TWEAKERS)

TURN IN
(BLONDE,
D)

Daisy Lowe's gothic-meets-vintage haven

Daisy is incredibly kind and generous, and through our shared love of colour we've developed a friendship I really cherish. Her distinctive style has been shaped by her mother, the fashion and textiles designer Pearl Lowe, along with her own incredible life experiences across the worlds of modelling and media. Having previously helped Pearl transform her coastal cabin in rural Sussex, England, I was delighted to help her daughter work on what has now become her own family home.

When I first visited Daisy she'd been living in the house for a while but was in the process of a major renovation, led by her property-developer fiancé Jordan, so it was a bit of a building site – which I love, as it means getting to work with blank canvas. Despite the building mayhem, you got an instant sense of Daisy's personality and tastes: everywhere you looked there were – in her words – 'mad old bits, weird and wonderful pieces and personal mementoes'. The house already told her story of where she's been and how she got there, so we needed to find the right colours to tie this all together and make it work for her next chapter.

Early on it became clear that pink needed to lead the scheme (although Daisy doesn't tend to wear this colour very much, she loves how uplifting it feels to be around). So pink tints and tones now feature in every room, through paint, furniture or accessories. To create a red thread, we used Pink 01 on all the skirting boards and door frames across the entire home, to emphasise pink as this core house colour.

But Daisy also wanted to hint at her beloved edgy, gothic influences, which we achieved by bringing in blacks and greys to temper it all down, alongside some grounding greens for a soothing feel. This began in her hallway, which was painted Pink

WHO LIVES HERE?

Daisy Lowe, a British model and media personality, her fiancé Jordan and their young daughter, Ivy.

INSTAGRAM

@daisylowe

THE PROPERTY

A stucco-fronted Georgian townhouse spread across three floors. The ground floor is a typical townhouse layout with a living room at the front leading off from the hallway, which has been knocked through into the original dining area and leads into their open plan kitchen. Upstairs is the couple's bedroom suite, incorporating a bathroom and walk-in dressing room. The third floor contains a guest room and Ivy's bedroom.

PREFERRED COLOURS AND STYLES

Soft greens with complementary pinks, dashes of cool grey and dramatic black accents to bring a little bit of edge.

04 across the walls (and of course, with Pink 01 skirting), with deep forest green featuring in her stair runner. Upstairs in her bedroom this palette is almost reversed, featuring a lighter sage tone (Green 09) on the walls for a more calming feel, while pink was introduced through her upholstered headboard rather than paint.

Back downstairs, Daisy wanted to go a little stronger and darker with her palette to create a cosy vibe, although she was initially nervous about it feeling heavy, especially in the living room. By using rich, saturated Grey 07 (which has a green undertone, so sits beautifully with its complementary-opposite pink) on all the living room walls, we created balance by keeping the window area light with Pink 01 on its shutters and other woodwork, creating nuances of light and dark.

The couple's kitchen underwent the biggest transformation by extending it out into the garden to create a much larger, social space which is now the true heart of the home and allows Daisy to indulge her love of cooking and socialising. Country-inspired elements are contrasted with contemporary touches (like her Belfast sink with luxe fluted detailing on its front), with a few bonus gothic nods, thrown in, too. We kept the walls light with Pink 02, to complement the deep, blue-toned green on the kitchen units, which reference the darker tones in the living room, as well as the greenery of the garden. And at night, when Daisy likes to light loads of candles, the way the light bounces off her treasured crockery and glassware feels really magical. It was a joy to help such a beautiful soul create a home that reflects everything that makes her so lovely.

Daisy's core house palette

KEY PARENT COLOURS

LEADING LICK PAINT PICKS

PINK 01   PINK 02   PINK 04   GREEN 02   GREEN 09   GREY 07

'Coming home to my pink hallway is such a joy – I open the door and it's like being greeted with a cuddle. Before moving here, I decorated my first home with loads of bright colours and patterns, so initially I thought I wanted this space to have a "grown-up" feel and was envisaging a plain and neutral palette.

But after my colour consultation with Tash, I realised the house really DID need colour. Adding all these lovely tones has been so transformative and every room feels so much warmer – really rich and cosy. It's totally changed the energy of the home – it's amazing you can create such a massive difference just through paint.'

- D A I S Y -

A final word

It's been such a treat to guide you through this process. As we come to the end, my biggest hope is that you now have the confidence to go ahead and create the colour-filled home of your dreams, whatever your own perfect palette may be (and speaking of which, make sure you go through the last of our Perfect Palette exercises on pages 222–223, which will help you collute everything we've discussed into one handy reference spot).

I truly believe that creating a beautiful home that makes your heart sing is less to do with budget or inherent 'good taste', and a lot more about knowing what's right for you and your home and having a clear idea of how to execute it with ease. I think that by now this goes without saying, but colour and design bring me so much joy, and even if you're not as interiors-mad as me, I hope you can see how nailing the look of your home can be a major source of happiness for both you and those you share the space with.

While this is (almost) the end of this book, I hope it's just the beginning of our relationship: I would LOVE you to join our lovely Lick community by engaging with me on Instagram (@tash_lickcolour) and tagging me in any of your own decorating posts, and my DMs are always open for any advice I can help you with.

Be sure to check out Lick.com, too, where we've got oodles of extra articles and videos full of decorating ideas and tips, as well as to find our full range of paints and tools.

Now, go forth and colour!

My go-to brands

Over the years I've ended up curating my own Little Black Book, which I wanted to share with you,. These are some of the tried-and-trusted brands, designers and artists I often turn to for furniture, fixtures and accessories to finish my clients' homes to perfection:

ART

I love using art to personalise a home – and I always think it looks really cool to mix in original paintings with contemporary prints and cool photography, for a layered look.

I've recommended the New York-based artist AndyBlank.com to many clients as I love his colourful, playful art prints (which are also really well priced). RiseArt.com is brilliant for discovering new, upcoming artists from artists around the world; but if you like keeping your options open, check out Interrupted.Art – this ingenious subscription service allows you to rent (rather than buy) art, meaning you can regularly switch up your look.

LIGHTING

Good lighting is crucial for how we see colour, and layering lighting helps create ambiance, but the aesthetics of our lights are equally important for finishing off a room scheme.

Pooky.com is one of my regularly-visited brands if I want to use beautifully patterned, colourful shades to coordinate with other patterns in that room, or for something more streamlined I'll often turn to Flos.com or LightsandLamps.com, for their modern-contemporary aesthetics.

FURNITURE

Comfort and quality are just as important as looks, especially for sofas and beds. Buy wisely and they can last a lifetime (with the occasional reupholstering, for a refreshed look).

The gorgeous corduroy sofa you might have seen on my Insta is by British brand JoandCoHome. com, and it's already been on several house moves with me. Its quality is amazing, especially for the price. Loaf (loaf.com) is another brand I love for its insanely comfy range of sofas and beds.

DCConcept.co.uk is a great one-stop shop for sourcing a vast range of contemporary and designer furniture products from different brands.

HARDWARE, FIXTURES AND MATERIALS

Whether you're renting or simply on a tight budget, I always encourage my clients to consider elevating existing built-in units rather than replacing them, where possible.

Try PlankHardware.com for stunning handles to transform kitchen cabinets, switch in some luxe new electrical fittings from DowsingandReynolds.com, or transform plain walls and cupboards with wooden panelling and decorative moulding – head to B&Q (diy.com) or HomeDepot.com for a huge range.

Decent faux wood flooring and cool stair runners can be hard to find, but FloorStreet.co.uk have a range of really premium looking engineered and laminate wood options – and I love the bold contrasting trims they offer on their runners, too.

ACCESSORIES

The jewellery of the home; if you want to finish off your scheme with some accent colour pops, add visual softness or bring in some quirky touches, these brands are my go-to's.

It's always such a treat to trawl the LateAfternoon. co.uk website – it's full of handcrafted pieces made by artisans, which all tell a story and bring instant character to your home. For more warm-neutral style pieces, ZaraHome.com has such a well curated selection of home accessories and furniture, which are so easy to bring into a variety of schemes.

The textile brand ColoursofArley.com are much-loved for their trademark bold striped patterns, which look perfect in any scheme – they're available as fabric, wallpaper and home accessories, so you can layer up colours and styles, or stick to a single statement accent. And if you love the boutique hotel look, SohoHome.com (who I've collaborated with on a number of Lick projects) sell furniture and accessories both used in, and inspired by, their stunning bars and hotels.

Community shout-out

To the incredible creators who shared their artistry within these pages — you are the true heart and soul of this book. Your willingness to open your homes and share your creative vision has made this collaboration not just possible, but an absolute joy.

The way you each approach colour and design with equal parts passion and playfulness resonates with millions across the globe who find daily inspiration in your work. I've been privileged to help tell just a small part of your story, but it's your collective creativity that brings these pages to life. Thank you for being such generous collaborators and for showing us all that home is wherever we dare to dream in colour.

I'd encourage all of you reading this book to head to these amazing contributors Instagram accounts — give them a follow and prepare to get massively inspired for your next decorating project:

Alanna Nicolex @groovyhousestudio
Amira Hashish @thedesigneditor
Aimée and Amanda @fettleandtinker
Alice Merritt @strikeme_pink
Alice @yarwoodatnumber41
Amie and Charlie @citytoseasidehome
Athena at Topology Interiors @topologyinteriors
Catherine Frost @53houseplantsandme
Chlo Hannant @chlohannant
Daisy Lowe @daisylowe
Dan McClark @mcclark_bespoke_kitchens
Danielle @the_house_on_the_grapevine
Elena @elemc_home
EMH London @emhlondon
Emil Eve Architects @emilevearchitects
Emily Rickard @emilyrickardstyle
Emma @homeonthegrove
Elizabeth Stanhope Design Studio
@elizabethstanhope
Felix Capital @felixcapital
Frances and Ben @itsnotsogrimupnorth
Gemma @lets.stay.at.home
Geri Dempsey @geridempsey
Hayley @kidofthevillage
Helen Ward @house.of.wards
Holly Christian @plucked_interiors

Jess Clark @charminglifebyjess
Jessica Elizabeth Horton @deorling_
Jim Chapman @jimchapman
Jo @maisonmilshaw
Joanna Landais at Eklektic Studio
@joannalandaisinteriors
Katie @aflickofpaint
Katie and Byron @buildbysets
Kay Train @kaytrainillustrator
Kelly @projectonrosslane
Laura and Adam @no5bristol
Laura Spencer @laura.elizabeth_
Lily and Tom @designinglilyspad
Lizzy Williams @renovationhq
Lucinda @thishovehome
Lucy Alice Home @lucyalicehome
Luke and Fran @number3_lcv
Margriet @bijmargrietinhuis
Marlena @with.marlena
Mary Charteris @marycharteris
Max at Newform Design & Build @newformdesign.uk
Michelle Kelly @kittykellystyle
Michelle Lognonné @maisonettemadness
Nat @100yearhouse
Nathalie and Timothy @imeanwhatcouldgowrong
Nicole Dennett @nicolejanelle
Nicki Bamford-Bowes @andthentheywentwild
Nick and Ant @studiototeda
Nothing is Not Nothing @nothingisnotnothing
Oak Furniture Land @oak_furniture_land
Reece Smith @littleedwardian
Roisin Quinn @roisinquinn
Rose Ashby @roseashbycooks
Sal @beyondtheblankcanvas
Sandra Dieckmann @sandradieckmann
Sara Austin @the_found_home
Sarah Aspinall @inside_number_5_
Sharn Rayment @sharnshouse
Steph @houseonthecorner_16
Stephanie Duckett @stephanieduckettceramics
Stephanie Elaine Tabor @setinteriors.studio
Sushma Samonini @house_on_the_way
Trish @interiorspickle
Trix Eden @trixedenbreuls
Victoria Covell @victoria_covell_interiors
Vita @belgravehome

Community shout-out

And a few special thank-yous to the amazing
photographers who allowed me to share their work
on these pages:

Amie Charlot @amiecharlot
Anna Stathaki @annastathakiphoto
Annie Kruntcheva @anniekrunchie
Beth Davis @_beth_davis
Chris Tubbs @christubbsphotography
Chris Wharton @chriswhartonphotography
Clara Molden @claramolden
David Cleveland @daveycleveland
Emma Lewis @emmalewisphotographer
Edward Conder @edwardconder
Elyse Kennedy @elysekennedy
Jon Aaron Green @jon_aaron_green_photographer
Leighton James @thepropertyphotographerltd
Oliver Perrott @oliverperrottphoto
Richard Kiely @_richardkiely
Ryan Tabor @ryantabro

Art Credits

The publisher has made every effort to credit all the
makers, artists and designers whose work appears
incidentally in the book and will be more than happy
to correct or add any omissions in future reprints.

Page 73, bottom left – The Mayor of Gravesend 1921-
1923, Alderman W.E. Thomas painted by James Clark
1858-1943
Page 149 – The Girl in the Yellow Hat, by Hannah
Nijsten @hannahnijsten
Page 190 – Cowboy Hat and Crab, by Layla Andrews
@laylandrews; Lou Reed at the Table, by Sam Smith
@jesuissamsmith
Page 194 – Lobster by Alice Peto @paintedbyalice
Page 224 – Safety Blanket by Sam Harris

Index

With thanks

Writing this book has certainly been a team effort, both in terms of its creation, and in getting me to this point where I'm now a published author! I'd like to take this moment to give my heartfelt thanks to some of the people who have helped me get here:

To the fantastic team at Lick, both past and present – without you, this book simply wouldn't exist!

To my colour angels, Sammy Bramley and Charlotte Cropper: the years working alongside these ladies were some of the best times of my life.

To all of my clients – thank you for letting me into your homes, and allowing me to include your beautiful spaces in this book.

To Joanna Thornhill – you are one of the most talented women I have had the pleasure of working with. Your patience and ability to translate my vision for this book into words has been invaluable in helping me turn all my thoughts and concepts into a cohesive story. One thing I didn't expect when I started working on this book was that I'd end up making a friend for life.

To Sophie Allen – from our very first meeting, I knew you were the best person to help me turn this project into a reality. Thank you for encouraging me to be myself. You've supported me throughout the entire process and been nothing short of my rock – I feel like I've learnt so much from you. I am forever grateful for your patience, especially while I've navigated juggling life as a new Mum.

To Katherine Case, thank you for your dedication and creativity. You have breathed life into the words on these pages in a way I would never have imagined. You've enabled me to explain nuances of colour and colour theory in an exciting, easy to digest way through your clever designs. I can't imagine this book without you!

And finally, to my amazing husband, Sam Bradley, for your love, support and for being my greatest inspiration.

About the author

As the Director of Interior Design at home decor brand Lick, Tash Bradley is not only the curator of Lick's distinctive colour collection, but to date, she has given colour consultations on over 5,000 rooms across the UK, EU and US, providing decorators the colour confidence they need to transform their houses into homes that they love.

Tash has spent her career working in the creative industry, first as a professional artist and then in the world of marketing. For over a decade, she has specialised in colour and interior design, working in property development and home decoration, as well as studying interior design at the University of Arts London. In the last 5 years, she has studied colour psychology and developed a personal colour theory that she shares with her clients.

Tash believes in the transformative power of colour as a tool for self-expression, communication, and happiness. Leveraging her expertise in colour psychology and theory, Tash helps people around the world find the colours that will positively impact not only their personal spaces but also their overall lifestyle and wellbeing. She is driven by her mission to help us understand colour, from the emotional reactions we have to it to how it impacts our everyday lives and shapes the space we call home.

Tash's unique approach to colour in design has established her as a trusted thought leader in the interiors world. Her expertise has been featured in *The Times, Architectural Digest, Homes & Gardens, ELLE Decor, Vogue, LivingEtc, House & Garden, The Telegraph, The Metro, Evening Standard, Stylist, The Independent, Ideal Home, Hello, Tatler, Daily Mail* and *Financial Times's How To Spend It.*

Quadrille, Penguin Random House UK, One Embassy Gardens, 8 Viaduct Gardens, London SW11 7BW

Quadrille Publishing Limited is part of the Penguin Random House group of companies whose addresses can be found at global. penguinrandomhouse.com

Copyright © Tash Bradley 2025
Photography © see individual captions
Illustrations © Loz Ives

Colour wheels on pages 25–26, 28, 30–34, 36–39, 43, 57, 133, 222 © adobe stock

Electronic equipment image on page 179 © adobe stock

Published by Quadrille in 2025

www.penguin.co.uk

A CIP catalogue record for this book is available from the British Library

ISBN 978-1-83783-204-0
10 9 8 7 6 5 4 3 2 1

Managing Director: Sarah Lavelle
Editorial Director: Sophie Allen
Content Producer/Editor: Joanna Thornhill
Copy Editor: Gaynor Sermon
Design: Katherine Case
Illustrator: Loz Ives
Senior Production Controller: Martina Georgieva
Production Director: Stephen Lang

Colour reproduction by F1

Printed in China by C&C Offset Printing Co., Ltd.

The authorised representative in the EEA is Penguin Random House Ireland, Morrison Chambers, 32 Nassau Street, Dublin D02 YH68.

Penguin Random House is committed to a sustainable future for our business, our readers and our planet. This book is made from Forest Stewardship Council® certified paper.